ARISTOTLE'S DEDUC

INDUCTION: INTRODUCTORY

ANALYSIS AND SYNTHESIS

© Editions Rodopi N.V., Amsterdam
Printed in the Netherlands
ISBN: 90–6203–228–1

TABLE OF CONTENTS

ARISTOTLE'S DEDUCTION AND INDUCTION: INTRODUCTORY ANALYSIS AND SYNTHESIS

Wayne N. Thompson

PREFACE

The origin of the present volume was a more general interest in Aristotle that the writer first pursued systematically in 1960 as a sabbatical project at the University of Illinois, Chicago Division. Later a half-time research grant for a semester at the University of Texas at Austin enabled him to continue his study of Aristotle's writings in the humanities and the social sciences that bear on rhetoric and communication.

Of the several topics comprising this general investigation, the analysis of Aristotle's logical system seems to many to be the one of greatest value. Several reasons lead to this judgment. First, the logical writings have been of unquestioned importance to Western civilization historically, and they continue to have significance. Second, even in translation the major writings are lengthy, tiresome, and difficult for modern readers. Third, existing commentaries deal more in scholarly argument than in clear, concise exposition. Fourth, Aristotle's works do not include a synthesis of his thoughts on induction.

The writer is grateful to those who have helped to make this book possible. Dr. Eugene Vest and Dr. H. W. Bailey were those initially responsible at the University of Illinois for the sabbatical leave. The person at the University of Texas the most helpful in arranging the leave was Dr. Jesse J. Villarreal.

Wayne N. Thompson
Houston, Texas, USA
May 24, 1974

CHAPTER I

Introduction and Purposes

The statement by Werner Jaeger that Aristotle "is the real father of logic"[1] may be an exaggeration, but it is not far from the literal truth. The earlier Greeks had treasured the exercising of the mind; and when Aristotle first became a student at Plato's Academy about 367 B.C., he found not only a substantial body of speculative thought but also a lively interest among his colleagues in dialectic as an intellectual sport. Nonexistent, though, was any systematic presentation of the principles of logic. Plato's writings contained no such treatment, and references to other ancient works do not indicate discussions of the subject by other scholars.

Aristotle's own writings also provide evidence, both positive and negative, of the deficiencies in earlier treatises. He charges his predecessors with neglecting the logical aspects of rhetoric[2] and of failing to examine causation clearly and completely.[3] For his work *On Sophistical Refutations* he claims total originality. "Of this inquiry," he says, ". . .it was not the case that part of the work had been thoroughly done before, while part had not. Nothing existed at all."[4] As for the *Topics,* the rules for dialectic encounter already existed, but Aristotle, so he claimed, was the first to codify them.[5]

Negative evidence on originality, which cannot be conclusive, also exists. Here the omission of passages mentioning earlier logical works is significant because of the frequency of such

1. *Aristotle: Fundamentals of the History of His Development,* tr. Richard Robinson (Oxford: At the Clarendon Press, 1948), p. 47.

2. *Rhetoric* i.l.1354^a 14.

3. *Metaphysics* i.7.988^{a}22 -23 and i.10.993^{a}10-15.

4. Ch. 34.183^{b}34 -36. The translation is by W. A. Pickard-Cambridge.

5. ". . .inasmuch, then, as we have no tradition bequeathed to us by others, let us try to say something upon the matter for ourselves." iii.5.159^a 37 -38. The translation is by W. A. Pickard-Cambridge.

citations in the other treatises. Chapters 3 -6 of the *Metaphysics,* Book i, contain a report on the work of previous thinkers. The first six chapters of the *Physics* contain numerous references to Parmenides, Melissus, Anaximander, Empedocles, Anaxagoras, and Democritus, and the sections on the infinite[6] and the void[7] begin with summaries of earlier opinions. *On the Soul* in its second chapter speaks of the importance of examining earlier works and then compares and contrasts the views of ten earlier writers or schools. The *Rhetoric* likewise begins with a comment on the deficiencies of earlier writers, and references to previous works appear frequently throughout the volume. Recognizing the importance of preceding writings, thus, was characteristic of Aristotle, and the absence of such comments in the *Organon* may possibly signify that nothing worth citing existed. Those references to other writers that do appear are identifications of sources of illustrations and do not indicate indebtedness for ideas.

But Aristotle is more than an originator historically significant. Modern works on logic and on argumentation attest to his continued importance. His Peripatetic successors added the hypothetical and the disjunctive syllogisms, but otherwise today's basic presentations of deduction are essentially Aristotelian. As for induction, his thoughts on this confused topic remain of interest. Perhaps Chapter 4 of this present work will be helpful in bringing some order to this muddled portion of logical theory.

That chapter, like the two that intervene, draws at times on the entire body of writings in the humanities and the social sciences, but the principal source is the *Organon.* The following is a brief summary of the volumes that compose this ancient work.

The *Categories* is a treatment of the terms from which statements are made. The work consists of an analysis of ten classes to which terms belong and of an examination of the simple relations of opposition, priority, and simultaneity.

On Interpretation, also a brief work, begins with an elementary treatment of grammar, but then Aristotle takes up the combining of terms into propositions.

The *Prior Analytics* is a detailed treatment of syllogisms.

6. iii. 4 -5.
7. iv.6.

The volumes include analyses of the figures, of the properties of the syllogism, of the defects of the syllogism, and of related matters. The volume is the basic work on deduction.

The *Posterior Analytics* is an application of the basic treatment to demonstrative or scientific thinking. This highest form of reasoning is based on premises that are certainties and that contain the causes.

The *Topics* is on deduction in dialectic. Unlike the first four books of the *Organon,* which are on reflective thought, the *Topics* is a guide to effective reasoning in situations involving communication with others. The first seven books are a vast number of commonplaces that give the student stock arguments for almost every conceivable point. Book viii is a handbook for the competitor, whose needs receive much more attention than do those of the dialectician searching with his colleagues cooperatively for truth. Premises in the dialectic syllogism are probabilities.

On Sophistical Refutations, a short work, is an analysis of the nature of fallacies (chs. 3 -15) and of the methods of exposing them (chs. 16 -32).

These six works, in conclusion, are the basic sources for the three chapters that follow. The writer's purposes in preparing this analysis and summary are the following:

1. To provide an introductory analysis of Aristotle's system of deduction so that the terminology and the essential features will be clear. To attain this objective, the writer has tried to select from a large body of complex material those features that are critical to the system. He also has tried to organize and express these ideas so that they will be clear to the modern reader. Studying the present volume should make it easier for the scholar who wishes to read the *Organon.*

2. To synthesize scattered materials on induction into a coherent, clearly stated system.

3. To give detailed citations and numerous footnotes so that the serious scholar can refer readily to translations of the original and to selected commentaries.

4. To take up some persistent issues, and to contribute some insights.

CHAPTER 2

The Nature and the Structure of Aristotle's Deduction

The preceding chapter closed with a statement of purposes that suggests the approach and the content of the pages that follow. Even in the best translations the involved thought, the profusion of detail, the compressed treatment, and the long, laborious sentences constitute formidable barriers for the modern student, and for most readers lack of background is still another handicap. A reasonably nontechnical introduction thus should be helpful even to the able scholar.

The organization of the chapter is into three parts. An introductory section gives an overview of Aristotle's logical system, including a section on levels of treatment. Next, the chapter contains an analysis of the anatomy of the syllogism. This section proceeds from a consideration of terms through an examination of the nature of premises to a study of the syllogism itself. Finally, there are sections on the manipulation of premises and on the role of causation.

TYPES OF REASONING

Aristotle's analysis of reasoning, unlike that of many modern textbooks, is in two parts. On this point there is consistency, for specific assertions about the twofold analysis occur in at least four different works – the *Prior Analytics,* the *Posterior Analytics,* the *Topics*, and the *Rhetoric.* These declarations are forthright: ". . . every belief comes either through syllogism or from induction."[1] ". . .we learn either by induction or by demonstration."[2] ". . .we must distinguish how many species there are of dialectical arguments. There is on the one hand Induction, on the other reasoning."[3] "As for real or apparent demonstration, there

1. *Prior Analytics* ii.23.68^{b}13 -14. The translation is by A. J. Jenkinson.
2. *Posterior Analytics* i.18.81^{a}39. The translation is by G. R. G. Mure. See also i.l.71^{a}3 -10.
3. *Topics* i.12.105^{a}10 -12. The translation is by W. A. Pickard-Cambridge.

are in Rhetoric two modes, corresponding to the two modes in Dialectic. . . . the example is a form of induction; while the enthymeme is a syllogism. . . . Whenever men in speaking effect persuasion through proofs, they do so either with examples or enthymemes; they use nothing else."[4]

The terms used for the two types of reasoning are not always the same and the precise meanings shift from one environment of thinking to another, but the basic distinction always is clear — induction is some sort of moving from particulars to a general stand, and deduction is the process of going from a major premise to a conclusion. These definitions, which are those commonly understood by most modern students, are adequate for this present introduction and analysis.

LEVEL OF TREATMENT

Most analyses of Aristotle's logical system are into two parts, scientific and nonscientific, with dialectic and rhetoric as subdivisions of the latter. The basic treatment of reasoning for all of these is in the *Categories, On Interpretation,* and the *Prior Analytics.* The *Posterior Analytics* adapts this basic system to the special requirements of scientific demonstration, and the *Topics* and the *Rhetoric* serve similar needs for dialectic and rhetoric respectively. The foregoing analysis omits eristic, whose treatment appears in *On Sophistical Refutations,* but this "false" or degenerate dialectic was relatively unimportant in Aristotle's writings and through the centuries has had only limited influence. One source of subject matter for dialectic, according to Aristotle, was *generally believed opinion,* whereas the material of eristic was *apparently generally believed opinion.*

The modern student also may disregard the following analysis in *On Sophistical Refutations:* "Of arguments in dialogue form there are four classes: Didactic, Dialectical, Examination arguments, and Contentious arguments."[5] These four are not coordinate, mutually exclusive types. Didactic and dialectical are major forms; the last two are special aspects of dialectic.

---

4. *Rhetoric i.2.1356*[a]*36 -*[b]*7.* The translation is by Lane Cooper.
5. Ch. 2.165[a]38 -[b]11. The translation is by W. A. Pickard-Cambridge.

The forms worthy of further attention, therefore, are demonstration, dialectic, and rhetoric. For these three it is worthwhile to examine the fundamental qualities and purposes of each in relation to the rigor required for premises and relationships. The consistency between purposes and rules is especially worth noting.

Purposes and Fundamental Qualities

The environment for scientific reasoning in Aristotle's system was abstract deliberation, and the objective was absolute truth. There was to be no compromising in content or method. Hence, the system required that all terms of any given syllogism be from the same genus and that they be necessary (incapable of being anything except what they are). The ultimate source for reasoning had to be the first principle of the particular science.

Much of man's thinking, however, occurs in circumstances that do not permit the application of the rigorous rules of scientific demonstration. Dialectic was an orderly method that the Greeks developed for reasoning about opinions generally believed. Its highest function was in the study of philosophical matters, but it also served in "casual encounters" and as an intellectual training device for the young men of the schools.[6] The rules were elaborate, but briefly the procedure was this. The respondent began the contest by choosing a thesis. The examiner then asked a series of questions, whose purpose was to secure premises from which he could construct a syllogism with a conclusion contradictory to the thesis. The assailant's questions had to be so phrased that the response would be the acceptance or the denial of a statement. Finally, if the questioner succeeded in submitting a syllogism contradictory to the thesis, the defendant had the opportunity to overthrow it by showing a fault in one of the premises or in the logic. The essential element in all of this was competition, and Aristotle's *Topics* consists of advice on how to succeed in these encounters.

Still different were the circumstances and the purposes for the practitioner of rhetoric. At this point the reader should keep in mind that a significant difference exists between the breadth of the rhetorical function in Aristotle and the breadth in contempor-

6. *Top.* i.2.101^{a}27 -37.

ary writings, such as those of Kenneth Burke. Whereas modern theorists see rhetoric as functioning in a great many situations and as utilizing many different means, Aristotle was writing about the speaker addressing an audience. The objective was persuasion, and discourse flowed in only one direction.

Rigor in Content and Manipulation

From the disparate natures and purposes just noted, further differences followed with consistency. One of these was in the source of the premises. For the distinction between demonstration and dialectic the *Prior Analytics* is clear:

> The demonstrative premiss differs from the dialectical, because the demonstrative premiss is the assertion of one of two contradictory statements (the demonstrator does not ask for his premiss, but lays it down), whereas the dialectical premiss depends on the adversary's choice between two contradictories.[7]

In Aristotle's rhetoric the source of premises was still different. Since the objective was persuasion, what really mattered was what happened in the mind of the listener. Whether the speaker verbalized the desired idea or induced its formulation by indirection was unimportant; finding the best of the available means of persuasion was the standard.

A second set of differences lay in the requirements for truth. In the field of scientific thought only true statements were admissible,[8] and they had to be formulated so that valid relationships were possible. In the intellectual exercise of dialectic, however, as the following passage indicates, credibility, not truth, was the standard:

> If our reasoning aims at gaining credence and so is merely dialectical, it is obvious that we have only to see that our inference is based on

7. i.1.24^{a}21 -25.

8. "By demonstration I mean a syllogism productive of scientific knowledge. . . . The premisses of demonstrated knowledge must be true, primary, immediate, better known than and prior to the conclusion, which is further related to them as effect to cause. . . . Syllogism there may indeed be without these conditions, but such syllogism, not being productive of scientific knowledge, will not be demonstration. The premisses must be true." *Post. An.* i.2.71^{b}17 -25.

premises as credible as possible. . . . If, however, one is aiming at truth, one must be guided by the real connexions of subjects and attributes.[9]

The meaning of "as credible as possible" is not clarified immediately, but passages elsewhere suggest that the tests are right method and competitive success rather than truth. In the portion of the work that obviously pertains to schoolboy competition the use of falsehoods is condoned and even encouraged:

> . . .since arguments of this kind are held not for the sake of instruction but for purposes of practice and examination, clearly one has to reason not only to true conclusions, but also to false ones, and not always through true premises, but sometimes through false as well. For often, when a true proposition is put forward, the dialectician is compelled to demolish it; and then false propositions have to be formulated. Sometimes also when a false proposition is put forward, it has to be demolished by means of false propositions.[10]

In the case of the *Rhetoric* the ethics of the work is a complex topic that require's a separate essay. Briefly, although Aristotle says that ". . .things that are true and things that are just have a natural tendency to prevail over their opposites,"[11] the overall nature of the work indicates that the primary test for premises is believability.

Third, differences in rigor are traceable to the three environments. In demonstration the formal rules for validity apply without exception; the objective is scientific truth, the reasoner has no motives other than finding truth or testing for it, and compromising with logical precepts is incompatible with the purposes.[12] In dialectic the same formal rules ostensibly apply and

---

9. *Ibid.*, i.19.81^{b}18 -23. The following passage from the opening of the *Topics* also contrasts demonstration with dialectic: "(*a*) [Reasoning] is a 'demonstration', when the premises from which the reasoning starts are true and primary, or are such that our knowledge of them has originally come through premises which are primary and true: (*b*) reasoning, on the other hand,is 'dialectical', if it reasons from opinions that are generally accepted. . . . those opinions are 'generally accepted' which are accepted by every one or by the majority or by the philosophers – i.e. by all, or by the majority, or by the most notable and illustrious." i.l. 100^{a}27 -^{b}22.

10. *Top.* viii.ll.161^{a}24-31.

11. i.l.1355^{a}21 -22. The translation is by W. Rhys Roberts.

12. "The proper object of unqualified scientific knowledge is something

knowledge of them is a valuable resource of the participants, but an error in structure prevents success only if detected. In rhetoric, also, the standards as compared with those for demonstration are relaxed. Although skill in reasoning again is valued, the ultimate test is whether the listener forms the desired relations among premises.

Similarly in induction, the topic for a later chapter, the differences in rigor are marked. In demonstration the generalization is acceptable only if it follows an examination of all particulars;[13] but in dialectic the questioner needs only to cite enough instances for the opponent to assent to the conclusion, and in rhetoric the test is whether the examples are likely to produce conviction.

Aristotle's logic, therefore, takes on special colorations in the three different environments. The major structural features, however, are the same for rhetoric and dialectic as for demonstration. The sections that follow are relevant to all subvarieties of Aristotle's deduction.

TERMS: THE SMALLEST ELEMENT IN DEDUCTION

Without proper terms, Aristotle shrewdly recognized, sound premises are impossible and the syllogistic process of putting premises together rests upon an unsatisfactory foundation. In the logical work the *Categories* he addresses himself to this initial problem.

Why the problem is fundamental becomes clear when one considers the nature of the syllogistic operation. The conclusion that A falls within C is true, because A falls within B and B within C; Socrates is proven to be mortal, because Socrates is a man and all men possess the quality of mortality. For this process to have validity A, B, and C must be precise terms, each with exact boundaries and each free from ambiguity.

The first step in dealing with the problem of terms was a recognition that definition may or may not be satisfactory. This

---

which cannot be other than it is." *Post. An.* i.2.71^{b}14 -16. See also i.6.74^{b}5 and i.33.88^{b}30 -34.

13. ". . .induction proceeds through an enumeration of all the cases." *Pr. An.* ii.23.68^{b}28 -29.

now seemingly elementary notion, original with Aristotle,[14] at the time was a profound discovery. So the *Categories* begins with a distinction between equivocal and univocal terms. In the former situation two objects have a common name but differing definitions, whereas "things are said to be named 'univocally' which have both the name and the definition answering to the name in common."[15] If both a real man and a figure in a picture are called "animal," the usage is equivocal because the definition of the man and the figure do not correspond; but if a man and an ox are both called "animal," the usage is univocal because the sense in which the two are animal is the same. Though this analysis appears repeatedly in the succeeding chapters, Aristotle does not clarify it further. The basic notions, nevertheless, are clear and salutary. The insistence that only univocal terms are acceptable in scientific reasoning directs attention to a vital problem, and the observation that words denote different orders of reality and that one must look beyond the word to what it signifies are doctrines that General Semanticists were to publicize twenty-three centuries later.

The possibilities for misusing words receives extended treatment in *On Sophistical Refutations,* which includes a description of six fallacies dependent on diction (ch. 4) and instruction on their refutation (chs. 19 -23). Summarized, Aristotle's advice is that the respondent signify the sense in which he is accepting or submitting a term. Still of interest is the analysis of one of the sources of difficulty:

> It is impossible in a discussion to bring in the actual things discussed: we use their names as symbols instead of them; and therefore we suppose that what follows in the names, follows in the things as well. . . . But the two cases (names and things) are not alike. For names are finite. . ., while things are infinite in number. Inevitably, then, . . .a single name [has] a number of meanings.[16]

Perceptiveness, good intention, and common sense are quali-

---

14. See George Grote, *Aristotle,* ed. Alexander Bain and G. C. Robertson (London, 1883), pp. 57 -58.

15. Ch. 1.1^{a}6 -8. The translation is by E. M. Edghill.

16. Ch. 1. 165^{a}5 -13.

ties that lead to proper terms, but devising more specific instruction was as difficult for Aristotle as it has been for all of his successors. His major attempt to deal with the problem is his system of categories. This is a system of ten headings,[17] and in theory every term belongs to one of these. Actually the headings are neither mutually exclusive nor all inclusive, and Aristotle himself does not give equal prominence to them. The discussions of substance, quantity, quality, and relation occupy separate chapters of the *Categories* (5 to 8 respectively), whereas the other six are barely mentioned in chapter 9. The following passage is Aristotle's list and set of illustrations:

> Expressions which are in no way composite signify substance, quantity, quality, relation, place, time, position, state, action, or affection. To sketch my meaning roughly, examples of substance are "man" or "the horse", of quantity, such terms as "two cubits long" or "three cubits long", of quality, such attributes as "white", "grammatical". "Double", "half", "greater", fall under the category of relation; "in the market place", "in the Lyceum", under that of place; "yesterday", "last year", under that of time. "Lying", "sitting", are terms indicating "position"; "shod", "armed", state; "to lance", "to cauterize", action; "to be lanced", "to be cauterized"; affection.[18]

The system of categories, despite its imperfections,[19] is useful in at least three ways. First, like the so-called commonplaces of dialectic and the *topoi* of rhetoric, it leads the mind to all of the different terms that are possible in a given situation — i.e., the reasoner by running down the set of categories can make sure that he overlooks no possiblity.

Second, the analysis dissects and illuminates the mechanism

17. Ten in the *Categories* and the *Topics,* but eight in some works.
18. Ch. $4.1^{b}25$ -$2^{a}4$.
19. Grote's evaluation is clear and astute: "[Aristotle] cannot keep [the categories] apart steadily and constantly; . . .the same predicate is referred to one head in one place, and to another head in another. . . . This is inevitable; for the predicates thus differently referred have really several different aspects, and may be classified in one way or another, according as you take them in this or that aspect. Moreover, this same difficulty of finding impassable lines of demarcation would still be felt, even if the Categories, instead of the full list of Ten, were reduced to the smaller list of the four principal Categories — Substance, Quantity, Quality, and Relation." P. 89.

of syllogistic reasoning. The term that serves as the subject of a premise must belong to the first category (substance), but not all substances belong to the same level — a fact vital to the choice and the arrangement of terms. "Frog, horse and man are not things in the same primary way as this frog, this horse or this man. The former are what Aristotle calls secondary substances."[20] Whereas primary substances can serve only as subjects, secondary can serve as predicates of the primary or as subjects of tertiary substances (e.g., animal). A secondary substance also can be the subject of a statement in which the predicate is a term belonging to any of the other nine categories. The basis of the whole system, however, is the primary substance. "Aristotle was, as far as we can see, original, in taking as the point of departure for this theory, the individual man, horse, or other perceivable object. . . . He thus stood opposed to the Pythagoreans and Platonists, who took their departure from the Universal."[21]

Third, the system of categories is useful in understanding and criticizing terms. If a term has predicates falling in more than one category, it is ambiguous or equivocal.[22] Moreover, certain qualities are true of all terms falling within a category, and hence knowledge of categories is knowledge of the individual term. For example, no substance has a contrary or can vary in degree, quantities have no contraries but most qualities do, and relatives always have correlatives with which they are interdependent.

Despite the usefulness of categories, ultimately, as stated previously, the reasoner must rely on his own good sense and resourcefulness. Two other specific features, however, are serviceable: for a syllogism to be valid, the three terms must be drawn from the same genus[23] and must belong to the same time. ". . .one cannot infer from an event which occurred in the past that a future event will occur. The reason of this is that the middle must be homogeneous, past when the extremes are past, future when they are future, coming to be when they are coming-to-be, actually existent when they are actually existent."[24]

20. Marjorie Grene, *A Portrait of Aristotle* (Chicago: University of Chicago Press, 1963), p. 76.
21. Grote, p. 97.
22. *Top.* i.15.107^{a}3 -17.
23. *Post. An.* i.7.75^{b}10 -20; i.23.84^{b}18 -19.
24. *Ibid.,* ii.12.95^{a}35 -38.

PREMISES: THE RELATION OF TERMS THROUGH PREDICATION

The creation of the univocal term (which may be a series of words provided that the words combine to form a single concept) is the first step toward the forming of a syllogism. The second step is the generation of the premise through the process of predication. This step brings two terms into a relationship. "A Premiss," says Aristotle, "is a sentence affirming or denying one thing of another."[25]

The format of the premise is simple and invariable in Aristotelian deduction:

First, a term serving as subject.

Second, a linking verb either asserting or denying the relation of subject and predicate.

Third, a second term to serve as predicate.

This process of predication, which sets forth two terms and their relationship, has the added significance of introducing the dimension of truth or acceptability. ". . .'man' and 'white', as isolated terms," Aristotle observes, "are not yet either true or false." ". . . there is no truth or falsity," he continues, "unless 'is' or 'is not' is added, either in the present tense or in some other tense."[26] Such statements, of course, do not mean that the choice of properly defined terms is unimportant to syllogizing; what they do say is that the creation of premises imposes new and different responsibilities. The reasoner at this stage must give full consideration to the truth of premises in demonstration, to their acceptability as opinion in dialectic, and to their persuasive values in rhetoric.

The detailed instruction on predication in *On Interpretation,* although its extensiveness shows that Aristotle regarded it as important, pertains only to the mechanism for truth and is not Aristotle's last word. As John Herman Randall, Jr., points out, the ultimate reliance is upon the power or faculty of knowing. Proposed premises are to be checked against the facts and examined dialectically, but even these steps are not the ultimate. "How do

25. *Pr. An.* i.1.24[a]15 -16.

26. *On Interpretation* Ch. 1.16[a]15 -18. The translation is by E. M. Edghill. See also Grote, pp. 109 -110.

we know that these *archai* (premises) are true? It is *nous* (the power of knowing), working with and in the midst of facts, working in the subject matter itself, that 'sees' the truth of the *archai.*"[27] "But those *archai* are established and validated as *archai*, not by reasoning or demonstration, but by *nous.*"[28]

Finally, the fact that the premise is an affirmation or a denial of a relationship and *can be nothing else* deserves emphasis, for upon this quality the whole mechanism of the syllogism rests. Not only is a question unacceptable as a premise but also a declarative sentence that takes a neutral stand blocks further deduction. The following passage is applicable to all formal syllogisms and not to dialectic alone:

> Not every universal question can form a dialectical proposition as ordinarily understood, e.g. "What is man? " or "How many meanings has 'the good'? " For a dialectical premiss must be of a form to which it is possible to reply "Yes" or "No", whereas to the aforesaid it is not possible.[29]

Types of Predicates

The premise, in Aristotelian language, consists of the predicate and that of which it is predicated. The number of types of predicate, according to the *Topics,* is four:[30] accident, genus, property, and definition.[31] Since the content is different in each type of predicate, the distinctions are of practical significance. Aristotle's definitions are as follows:

"A 'definition' is a phrase signifying a thing's essence."[32] It may define either a term or another phrase.

27. *Aristotle* (New York: Columbia University Press, 1960), p. 44.

28. *Ibid.,* p. 46.

29. *Top.* viii.2.158^{a}14 -17. *On Interpretation* makes the same point, though not so directly: ". . .it is plain that a question of the form 'what is it?' is not a dialectical question, for a dialectical questioner must by the form of his question give his opponent the chance of announcing one of two alternatives, whichever he wishes." Ch.11.20^{b}26 -29.

30. In i.8 Aristotle gives two proofs that these are the only types of predicate. The passage reads in part: ". . .if any one were to survey propositions and problems one by one, it would be seen that each was formed either from the definition of something or from its property or from its genus or from its accident." The second confirmation is through reasoning. 103^{b}3 -19.

31. *Ibid.,* i.4.101^{b}24 -25.

32. *Ibid.,* i.5.101^{b}38 -39.

"A 'property' is a predicate which does not indicate the essence of a thing, but yet belongs to that thing alone, and is predicated convertibly of it. Thus it is a property of man to be capable of learning grammar."[33]

A genus is the "reply to the question, 'What is the object before you? '; as, for example, in the case of man, if asked that question, it is appropriate to say 'He is an animal'."[34]

"An 'accident' is (1) something which, though it is none of the foregoing − i.e. neither a definition nor a property nor a genus − yet belongs to the thing: (2) something which may possibly either belong or not belong."[35] The second definition, so Aristotle says, is the better of the two, "[for it] is sufficient of itself to tell us the essential meaning of the term in question."[36] An accident, thus, is a quality that is true of the subject but only at times. "Sitting" is an accidental attribute of man, and some objects may be white at times and not at others.

This analysis of the types of predication is of great importance to Aristotelian theory, for each of the four has its own set of characteristics and requirements. The treatment of these is in the *Topics*, Books ii-vii. In these books the dominating viewpoint is that of the questioner, and consequently the content is largely a detailed catalogue of possible errors − i.e., of opportunities for attack. However, since this advice arises out of the special and inherent characteristics of each of the four types, the lines of attack may be viewed also as an exposition of the necessary characteristics of each type of predication. Moreover, since this instruction deals largely with formal factors and since formal factors are applicable to all types of syllogism, the advice on predication is pertinent to all levels of deduction. Finally, since showing predication to be faulty is the same as showing the premise to be faulty, this detailed analysis in Books ii-vii deals with matters critical to syllogistic validity.

The rules themselves concerning the four types of predicate are beyond the scope of this introduction, but the role of categories should be mentioned. These, as already pointed out, are

33. *Ibid.* , i.5.102^{a}17 -20.
34. *Ibid.,* i.5.102^{a}33 -36. Aristotle's definition of genus reads, "A 'genus' is what is predicated in the category of essence of a number of things exhibiting differences in kind." i.5.102^{a}31 -32.
35. *Ibid.,* i.5.102^{b}4 -6.
36. *Ibid.,* i.5.102^{b}13 -14.

useful in generating and criticizing terms and thus are vital to the process of predication. Aristotle, moreover, utilizes the categories in his exposition of the four predicables. "The classes of predicates," he says, "are ten in number: Essence, Quantity, Quality, Relation, Place, Time, Position, State, Activity, Passivity." "For the accident and genus and property and definition of anything," he continues, "will always be in one of these categories."[37] In the *Posterior Analytics,* also, Aristotle falls back upon the system of categories in his "prefatory remarks" on "predicates generally." At this point he applies his analysis of the different types of substance as well as the whole notion of categories.[38]

Premises, thus, are a step beyond terms in the formulation of the syllogism and are unlike terms in that truth or appropriateness is a consideration. Structurally they consist of a subject, a verb asserting or denying, and a predicate.

Types of Premises

The nature of the terms and their relations to one another produce a number of types of premise. Whether a syllogism is valid depends in part on the type of premise, but the major purpose at present is not to probe the complexities of deduction but to provide the vocabulary required for beginning a study of this system.

First, premises are universal, particular, or indefinite.[39]

---

37. *Ibid.,* i.9.103^{b}20 -25. See also *Pr. An.* i.37. 49^{a}6 -10.

38. See i.22.83^{a}19 -^{b}17. One portion of this chapter reads, ". . .every predication displays the subject as somehow qualified or quantified or as characterized under one of the other adjectival categories, or else is an element in its substantial nature: these latter are limited in number, and the number of the widest kinds under which predications fall is also limited, for every predication must exhibit its subject as somehow qualified, quantified, essentially related, acting or suffering, or in some place or at some time." ^{b}13 -17.

39. This is the analysis in the *Prior Analytics.* The division in *On Interpretation* is between universal and individual. "By the term 'universal' I mean that which is of such a nature as to be predicated of many subjects, by 'individual' that which is not thus predicated. Thus 'man' is universal, 'Callias' an individual. Our propositions necessarily sometimes concern a universal subject, sometimes an individual." Ch.7.17^{a}38 -^{b}2.

Universal means that the predicate belongs to all instances of the subject or to none (all men are mortal; no man is divine); particular, that the predicate belongs to some instances of the subject but not to others (some men have red hair); indefinite that whether universal or particular cannot be determined (pleasure is not good).[40] In the elaboration of the system only universal and particular are important, because in many places Aristotle considers only the two and because the indefinite when considered does not have its own rules but follows those for the particular.

Second, premises are affirmative or negative.[41] This qualitative characteristic, which employs *affirmative* and *negative* in their ordinary senses, combines with the quantitative to produce four types of premise – universal affirmative, universal negative, particular affirmative, particular negative.[42]

Third, premises may be true or false. This characteristic has no bearing on the validity of the syllogistic process, but Aristotle's inclusion of this dimension is worth noting. The widely held idea that he restricted his treatment of syllogism to formal aspects is incorrect. To be demonstrative, he says, a premise must be both "true and obtained through the first principles of its science."[43] At this point Aristotle does not define *true,* but his works generally indicate that he believed that verbal statement and reality should be consistent.[44] The inclusion of causation as a vital part of deduction was an important attempt to make syllogisms factually true as well as formally valid (see closing section of

40. *Pr. An.* i.1.24^{a}16 -21.

41. *Ibid.,* i.2.25^{a}2 -3.

42. Although a negative premise may lead to a valid conclusion in some figures, Aristotle devotes one chapter of the *Posterior Analytics* to arguing that affirmative demonstration excels negative. He gives four reasons. See i.25.

43. *Pr. An.* i.1.24^{a}30 -31.

44. '. . .he who thinks the separated to be separated and the combined to be combined has the truth, while he whose thought is in a state contrary to that of the objects is in error." *Metaphysics* ix.10.1051^{b}3 -5. The translation is by W. D. Ross. The point that truth depends on the proper combination or separation of terms appears so often that the importance to Aristotle of the analysis seems clear. See *Ibid.,* 1052^{b}34 -35; *ibid.,* vi.4.1027^{b}17 -30; *On Int.* Ch. 1.16^{a}11 -12.

chapter), and some of the materials on induction also pertain to factual truth (see Chapter 4). Of lesser importance are a small number of observations widely scattered through the corpus. "With a true view all the data harmonize," he states in the *Nicomachean Ethics,* "but with a false one the facts soon clash."[45] Approaching the task of finding truth negatively, he warns that "Popular acceptance or rejection is no criterion of a basic truth"[46] and that "... appearances may mislead."[47]

False premises, as well as equivocal terms, it is interesting to note, can lead to true conclusions. Just as the term when taken in one sense may permit a true conclusion but when taken in a second way may produce one that is false,[48] so may a correct outcome occur, though by accident, when one premise or both are false.[49] The full analysis of the effects of false premises on the conclusion is exhaustive.

Fourth, premises may be necessary, assertoric, or contingent.[50] Simply explained, these differences reside in the verb connecting the two terms of a premise. Necessity arises from an *is necessarily* relation, simple assertion from an *is* relation, and contingency from a *may be* or *may not be* relation. Aristotle introduces this treatment[51] with the following words:

> Since there is a difference according as something belongs, necessarily belongs, or may belong to something else. . ., it is clear that there will be different syllogisms to prove each of these relations, and syllogisms with differently related terms, one syllogism concluding from what is necessary, another from what is, a third from what is possible.[52]

Fortunately, the matter is less complex than the final part of the passage predicts, for many of the syllogistic rules do not change as the universal affirmative, universal negative, particular affirmative,

45. i.8.1098^{b}11 -12.

46. *Post. An.* i.6.74^{b}23 -24.

47. *Meta.* iv.5.1010^{b}1 -29.

48. *On Int.* Ch. 8.18^{a}16 -27.

49. *Pr. An.* ii.2.53^{b}4 -4.57^{b}17.

50. Translators and commentators do not use consistent nomenclature for these three types. Another term for *necessary* is *apodictic*; for *assertoric, pure*; for *contingent, problematic* or *possible.*

51. *Pr. An.* i.8 -22.

52. *Ibid.,* i.8.29^{b}29 -35.

and particular negative premises assume the necessary, assertory, or contingent modes. Even so, the problem of analyzing the various combinations is a tedious one. The number of possible syllogisms is 432 (12 types of major premises x 12 types of minor premises x 3 figures). Fourteen chapters of the *Prior Analytics* (chs. 9 -22) contain analyses of many of the possibilities.

Of these three modes, the necessary was of special interest to Aristotle because the demonstration is valid only if one of the two premises meets this requirement. But what is meant by *necessity*, and how does the reasoner test for it? At some points Aristotle sets forth three conditions, any one of which indicates necessity. In the *Metaphysics* he states, ". . .that which is necessary perforce because it is contrary to natural impulse, that without which the good is impossible, and that which cannot be otherwise but can exist only in a single way."[53] In another place, though, a threefold definition is accompanied by the observation that the first two are derived from the third,[54] and elsewhere it is clear that it is the third concept that he really relies on. ". . .this is what 'being necessary' means — that it is impossible for the thing not to be," he states in the *Metaphysics* at iv.4.1006^{b}32 -33. ". . .that which cannot be otherwise is necessarily as it is" appears a little later at v.6.1015^{a}34 -35, and still other wordings appear elsewhere.

Even with such a clear-cut definition, testing a particular premise for necessity is difficult. Scattered through the corpus are brief attempts to relate necessity to such fundamental parts of the Aristotelian system as actuality-potentiality,[55] the four kinds of cause,[56] and the distinction between events caused by nature and those caused by chance, but these do not produce usable guides for testing necessity.

The most important method of expanding the definition is the contrast with accident. This contrast appears in several places without much change in content or even in the examples. Univer-

53. xii.7.1072^{b}11 -13.

54. *Ibid.*, v.5.1015^{a}20 -35.

55. For example, see *On Int.* Ch. 9.18^{b}10 -16; and *On Generation and Corruption* ii.11.337^{b}10 -338^{b}6. The translation is by H. H. Joachim.

56. For example, see *Phys.* ii.9.199^{b}34 -200^{a}14. The translation is by R. P. Hardie and R. K. Gaye.

sality of occurrence and the presence of a cause making the event inevitable are the principal criteria:

> Since, among things which are, some are always in the same state and are of necessity. . ., and some are not of necessity nor always, but for the most part, this is the principle and this the cause of the existence of the accidental; for that which is neither always nor for the most part, we call accidental. . . . To accidental results there corresponds no determinate art nor faculty; for of things which are or come to be by accident, the cause also is accidental. . . . The matter, therefore, which is capable of being otherwise than as it usually is, must be the cause of the accidental.[57]

Fifth, still other terms that describe certain features of premises are important to the vocabulary of the reader, though not significant to the formal analysis of the syllogism. A *hypothesis* must be acceptable to the pupil and "capable of proof but assumed by the teacher without proof."[58] If not acceptable to the pupil, it is a *postulate.*[59] *Primary* premises, also known as *immediate*, are basic truths whose origins are not by prior demonstration. "In saying that the premises of demonstrated knowledge must be primary, I mean that they must be the 'appropriate' basic truths, for I identify primary premiss and basic truth. A 'basic truth' in a demonstration is an immediate proposition. An immediate proposition is one which has no other proposition prior to it."[60] *Commensurately universal,* a characteristic essential to demonstration, means invariably related: "I term 'commensurately universal' an attribute which belongs to every instance of its subject, and to every instance essentially as such; from which it clearly follows that all commensurate universals inhere *necessarily* in their subjects. . . .An attribute belongs commensurately and universally to a subject when it can be shown to belong to any random instance of that subject and when the subject is the first thing to which it can be shown to belong."[61]

57. *Meta.* vi.2.1026^{b}27 -1027^{a}15; see also v.30.1025 ^{a}13 -29 and xi.8. 1064^{b}30 -1065^{a}2.

58. *Post. An.* i.2.76^{b}27 -28.

59. *Ibid.,* 76^{b}30 -31.

60. *Ibid.,* i.2.72^{a}5-8. Also: ". . . knowledge of the immediate premisses is independent of demonstration." *Ibid.,* i.3.72^{b}19 -20.

61. *Ibid.,* i.4.73^{b}26 -33. The italics appear in the translation.

Conclusion

The number of possible types of premises, all created through predication, is extremely large, and many of these possess qualities that affect the validity of the total syllogistic process. To discuss the premise and the syllogism separately is artificial, but unavoidable. Perhaps the preceding attempt to explain the nature of the premise and to introduce the needed terminology will be helpful as a preliminary to the study of the Aristotelian treatment of how premises are related.

RELATION OF PREMISES: THE SYLLOGISM

Only preliminary are the invention of terms and the formulation of premises through predication; the verification or the refutation of a thesis and the deduction of new knowledge depend upon the syllogism.[62] Grote observes that in moving from *On Interpretation* to the *Prior Analytics,* "We pass now from the region of *declared* truth, into that of inferential or *reasoned* truth. We find the proposition looked at, not merely as communicating truth in itself, but as generating and helping to guarantee certain ulterior propositions, which communicate something additional or different."[63] To infer something additional, two premises are essential: ". . .the positing of one thing — be it one term or one premiss — never involves a necessary consequent: two premisses constitute the first and smallest foundation for drawing a conclusion."[64]

Qualities Common to All Syllogisms

The possible types of premises and conclusions are numerous, as the preceding discussion suggests, but some qualities are common to all groups of statements that deserve the name

---

62. "A syllogism is discourse in which, certain things being stated, something other than what is stated follows of necessity from their being so. I mean by the last phrase that they produce the consequence, and by this, that no further term is required from without in order to make the consequences necessary." *Pr. An.* i.1.24^{b}18-20. Randall maintains that the syllogism was not a means of deducing new knowledge. P. 40 *et passim.*

63. P. 141.

64. *Post. An.* i.3.73^{a}8-11. See also *Pr. An.* i.15.34^{a}17-18 and i.23.40^{b}35-37.

syllogism. First, in the Aristotelian system, which has only the categorical form, the premises and the conclusions are declarations affirming or denying that one term belongs to another. Second, the syllogism always consists of three statements – a major premise, a minor premise, and a conclusion:

> All men are mortal.
> Socrates is a man.
> Therefore, Socrates is mortal.

Fewer than three statements may be expressed, but such shortcuts do not alter the number of sentences forming the *actual* unit of thought. Similarly, more than three statements may be combined in discourse, but in this instance the reasoning is a series of two or more syllogisms in which at least one premise in the final one is proven through another syllogism that is preliminary.[65] Informality in expression, which may be highly desirable rhetorically, does not relieve the reasoner of the responsibility for relating the premises correctly in each of the syllogisms forming the unit. Third, the syllogism always consists of three terms, each of which appears twice. In each appearance the concept that the word represents must be the same – i.e., each term must be univocal.

Figures and Modes

Still other factors important to the analysis of deductive validity are figures and modes.

Although four figures are possible,[66] Aristotle considers only three. In the first the middle term is the subject of the major premise and the predicate of the minor; in the second the middle term is the predicate in both premises; and in the third it is the subject in both.[67] The nature of the premises – whether true or false, affirmative or negative, universal or particular, or assertoric, necessary, or contingent – it should be noted, has no bearing on the classification by figures; only the position of the middle term

65. For a discussion of situations in which the number of statements is more or less than three, see *Pr. An.* i.31.47[a]10 -24.

66. In the fourth figure the middle term would be the predicate of the major premise and the subject of the minor.

67. Among the places where these analyses appear is *Pr. An.* i.32.47[b]1 -7. See also *ibid.,* i.4.25[b]31 -35, i.5. 26[b]33 -39, and i.6.28[a]10 -14.

is significant. In all figures the middle term must appear in both premises. It is the means by which the extremes are connected and through which proof takes place.[68]

Each figure has sixteen modes, and the Aristotelian analysis of validity depends upon this classification of syllogisms into forty-eight possible forms.[69] As stated earlier, the major premise may be universal affirmative, universal negative, particular affirmative, and particular negative, and the sixteen modes arise out of the combinations of these four with the same four possible minor premises. Four modes produce valid conclusions in the first figure, four in the second, and six in the third. For the conclusion to be valid the following criteria must be met for the respective figures:

In the first figure the major premise must be universal, and the minor must be affirmative.

In the second figure the major premise must be universal, and one premise must be negative. The only valid conclusions are negative.

In the third figure at least one premise must be universal. The only valid conclusions are particular.

Laws of Thought

Basic to the entire system, according to Post-Aristotelian analyses, are three presuppositions:

The Law of Identity: A term must mean the same in all parts of the syllogism.

The Law of Contradiction: Something cannot both be and not be at the same time.

The Law of Excluded Middle: All instances belong to one or the other of the opposites.

The first of these laws is the requirement for univocality, whose basic treatment is in the *Categories.* The second[70] and the

68. *Ibid.,* ii.19.66^{a}28 -29; *Post. An.* i.23.84^{b}23; ii.6.92^{a}10; ii.11. 94^{a}25 -26.

69. For the basic analysis, see *ibid.,* i.4 -6. The application of this analysis to the various combinations of assertoric, necessary, and contingent premises is in chs. 8 -22.

70. Esp. iv.3.1005^{b}18 -iv.6.1011^{b}23 and xi.5.1061^{b}34 -1062^{b}11. Much of this material is a consideration of objections to the Law of Contradiction. Perhaps the two best brief statements of the Law are these: ". . .the **same**

third[71] occupy most of Book iv and Book xi, chapters 4 -6, of the *Metaphysics.*

Important as these three laws are, they are not strictly applicable to the reasoning that occurs in many circumstances. Nor does Aristotle call for their extension to all deduction, as some misinformed critics charge. Particularly noteworthy are the far-ranging exceptions to the Law of the Excluded Middle. Indeed, intermediates are prominent in the total system. The *Categories,* chapter 6, specifically distinguishes between discrete and continuous quantity,[72] the notion of the intermediate is basic to the analysis of the emotions in the *Ethics,* and the Golden Mean appears in many places throughout the corpus.

Contraries and Contradictories

Also basic to deductive theory is the distinction between contraries and contradictories, still another of Aristotle's contributions. "The distinction of Contradictory and Contrary," Grote states, "is fundamental in ratiocinative Logic, and lies at the bottom of the syllogistic theory as delivered in the Analytica Priora."[73] The reason for this statement is that without the distinction subtle logical errors whose avoidance is vital to the expression of true premises go unnoticed.

Although references to contraries and contradictories appear in such widely different works as the *Nicomachean Ethics,* the *Metaphysics,* the *Physics,* the *Rhetoric,* and each of the six volumes of the *Organon,* the present concern is with the differ-

---

attribute cannot at the same time belong and not belong to the same subject and in the same respect" (iv.3.1005^{b}18 -20); ". . .the most indisputable of all beliefs is that contradictory statements are not at the same time true" (iv.6.1011^{b}12-14). These statements are respectively near the beginning and the end of the treatment of the Law in Book iv; Book xi generally is regarded as a brief version of iv.

71. Esp. iv.7.1011^{b}23 -1012^{a}28. ". . .there cannot be an intermediate between contradictories, but of one subject we must either affirm or deny any one predicate."

72. Also: "This is why in some cases there is a mean (there are men who are neither good nor bad), and in others there is not (a number must be odd or even)." *Ibid.,* x.4.1055^{b}23 -25.

73. P.137.

ences between the two as they apply in logic. First, though, a brief statement about contraries is desirable.

The treatment, of course, has different emphases and kinds of significance in the various Aristotelian works, but the basic idea is essentially constant. The following passage in the *Categories* provides the context for the material on contraries in that work:

> Things are said to be opposed in four senses: (i) as correlatives to one another, (ii) as contraries to one another, (iii) as privatives to positives, (iv) as affirmatives to negatives. Let me sketch my meaning in outline. An instance of the use of the word "opposite" with reference to correlatives is afforded by the expressions "double" and "half"; with reference to contraries by "bad" and "good". Opposites in the sense of "privatives" and "positives" are "blindness" and "sight"; in the sense of affirmatives and negatives, the propositions "he sits", "he does not sit".[74]

The passage continues by offering as illustrations of contraries "good" and "bad," "healthy" and "ill," "odd" and "even," and "black" and "white."[75] These examples, which are imbedded in a discussion dealing largely with which kinds of contraries have intermediates, are consistent with the more detailed and sophisticated analyses in the *Metaphysics.* The two things that are contrary are those that have the greatest difference and whose difference is complete. These are the extremes of a series, beyond whose ends there is nothing.[76] The following passage elaborates:

> The term "contrary" is applied (1) to those attributes differing in genus which cannot belong at the same time to the same subject, (2) to the most different of the things in the same genus, (3) to the most different of the attributes in the same recipient subject, (4) to the most different of the things that fall under the same faculty, (5) to the things whose difference is greatest either absolutely or in genus or in species. The other things that are called contrary are so called, some because they possess contraries of the above kind, some because they

74. Ch.10.11[b]15 -23. The remainder of the chapter explains each of these four in detail.

75. Ch. 10.12[a]1-25.

76. *Met.* x.4.1055[a]4 -18. The same thought appears in several works. ". . .those things are contraries which, within the same class, are separated *by the greatest possible distance." Cat.* Ch. 6.6[a]17 -19. See also *Nicomachean Ethics* ii.8.1108[b]26 -35. The translation is by W. D. Ross.

are receptive of such, some because they are productive of or suscepti-
ble to such, or are producing or suffering them, or are losses or
acquisitions, or possessions or privations, of such.[77]

This explication is of considerable use in setting out circumstances
in which "most differences" arise and in pointing to methods of
reaching contraries through reasoning, but within these various
areas, such as two cases within a particular genus, the individual
ultimately is thrown back upon his own judgment about which
qualities are the extremes or are at the greatest distance.

This notion of bipolarity as a characteristic of much that
concerned and surrounded man, though posing difficulties in application and raising knotty problems in theorizing,[78] is useful to
Aristotle in many ways. Contrariety is a property considered in
analyzing substance and the other categories, it is an explanatory
principle recurring frequently in the *Metaphysics,* and it is of
some, though lesser, importance in the *Physics.* The *Rhetoric* cites
the use of a contrary statement as one of the four general methods
of refutation,[79] and makes the more general concept of opposites
the first of the twenty-eight topoi.[80] References to contraries
appear so often in the *Topics* that the conclusion is justified that in
Aristotle's mind knowing how to apply them facilely in dialectic
discourse was essential to survival in competition.[81]

Also essential to the reasoner is a grasp of the nature of
contradictories, which Aristotle defined by writing, "Those positive and negative propositions are said to be contradictory which
have the same subject and predicate."[82] Unlike contraries, contradictories have no intermediate;[83] and whereas a statement may

---

77. *Met.* v. 10.1018^{a}25 -35.

78. Important among these is the rather illuminating series of attempts to
distinguish between contrariety and the other forms of opposition (esp. *Cat.*
Ch. 10 and *Meta.* x.4.1055^{a}33 -^{b}29) and the involved efforts at dealing with
contraries as related to their intermediates (esp. *Cat.* Ch. 10.12^{a}1 -25 and
Meta. x.7.1057^{a}18 -^{b}34).

79. ii.25.1402^{a}34 -37; ^{b}3 -6.

80. "One line of positive proof is based upon consideration of the opposite of the thing in question.... 'Temperance is beneficial; for licen-
tiousness is hurtful'." ii.23. 1397^{a}6 -11. The translation is by Roberts.

81. See esp. ii.7, ii.8, iv.3, v.6, vi.9, vii.3, and viii.13.

82. *On Int.* Ch. 6.17^{a}33 -35.

83. *Post. An.* i.2.72^{a}12 -13.

have more than one contrary, it can have only one contradictory.[84] Such sharply defined qualities make this type of opposite very useful in precise reasoning, but one attribute produces complications. Unlike contraries, the statements are not always universals:

> An affirmation is opposed to a denial in the sense which I denote by the term "contradictory", when, while the subject remains the same, the affirmation is of universal character and the denial is not. The affirmation "every man is white" is the *contradictory* of the denial "not every man is white", or again, the proposition "no man is white" is the contradictory of the proposition "some men are white". But propositions are opposed as *contraries* when both the affirmation and the denial are universal, as in the sentences "every man is white", "no man is white", "every man is just", "no man is just".[85]

This possible lack of universality means that in some units of reasoning the use of contradictories is indecisive — i.e., proving one member of a pair true does not always prove its opposite to be false. Only if three conditions are met is it certain that the one contradictory is true and the other false:

1. The statement must be universal or individual.

2. The time must be past or present.

3. The syllogism must not be contingent.[86]

The different kinds of opposites,[87] including contraries and contradictories, in conclusion, are important to Aristotle's logical system. The following passage in the *Prior Analytics* summarizes his views on the importance of the latter:

> It is clear then that not the contrary but the contradictory ought to be supposed in all the syllogisms. For thus we shall have necessity of inference, and the claim we make is one that will be generally accepted. For if of everything one or other of two contradictory statements holds good, then if it is proved that the negation does not hold, the

84. *On Int.* Ch.10.20[b]3 -4.

85. *Ibid.,* Ch. 7.17[b]15 -23.

86. *Ibid.,* Ch. 7.17[b]28 -34; Ch. 9.18[a]28 -33.

87. A full treatment of Aristotle's opposites seems beyond the scope of this chapter and irrelevant to its essential purpose. The other types of opposition are (1) affirmation and negation, (2) correlatives, and (3) positives and privatives. The general treatment is in *Cat.* Ch. 10.

affirmation must be true. Again if it is not admitted that tl
tion is true, the claim that the negation is true will be
accepted. But in neither way does it suit to maintain the *con*
it is not necessary that if the universal negative is false, the
affirmative should be true, nor is it generally accepted that if t
false the other is true.[88]

MANIPULATION OF PREMISES

Logic is a dynamic process, and Aristotle's deduction is a
system possessing variety and flexibility. Although the proper
procedures, at least in demonstration, are precise and unbending,
the total number of valid possibilities is considerable. The pages
that follow are an introduction to the rules and the methods.

Formal Rules

To be followed strictly in demonstration, the formal rules
are useful to dialectician and orator, but not universally and
invariably. In nonscientific thought the rules help the practitioner
to function with greater facility, and they also help him to detect
and avoid errors. In rhetoric using sound logic also may enable the
speaker to share in the persuasive power natural to truth. The
result in rhetoric, though, is more important than method, and
both the kinds of materials and the standards demanded by
audiences make relaxations of formal requirements permissible.

Aristotle's own presentation of the rules for the syllogism,
complicated by the inclusion of detailed proofs and arguments, is
an exhaustive exposition of deductive logic. The following list is
both a guide for those who wish to examine the topic further in
Aristotle and an elementary summary for those who do not. To
begin, probably all readers know that a syllogism has three terms
and that it has two premises, but it may not be known that
Aristotle states these requirements himself and that they are not
the work of later analysts. "So it is clear that every demonstration
and every syllogism will proceed through three terms only," he
says in the *Prior Analytics*; and immediately thereafter he states,
". . .it is clear that a syllogistic conclusion follows from two
premisses and not from more than two."[89] The other most
important rules are as follows:

88. ii.11.62^{a}10.
89. i.25.42 ^{a}30 -32.

1. To be valid a syllogism must have one premise that is affirmative. "Further in every syllogism one of the premisses must be affirmative."[90]

2. To be valid a syllogism must have one premise that is universal. ". . .unless one of the premisses is universal either a syllogism will not be possible, or it will not refer to the subject proposed, or the original position will be begged."[91]

3. All valid conclusions in the second figure are negative.[92]

4. All valid conclusions in the third figure are particular.[93]

5. ". . .a simple conclusion is not reached unless both premisses are simple assertions, but a necessary conclusion is possible although one only of the premisses is necessary."[94] Necessity results, however, only under certain conditions that chapters 9 -11 of the *Prior Analytics* identify.

5a. In the first figure, the major premise must be necessary;[95] if one premise is particular, the universal premise is the one that must be necessary.[96]

5b. In the second figure, the negative premise must be necessary.[97]

5c. In the third figure, if both premises are affirmative, a universal must be necessary;[98] and if only one is affirmative, a negative universal must be necessary for the conclusion to be necessary.[99]

6. When one premise or both premises state possibilities, the relation of premises to conclusion involves special rules. Factors bearing on the nature of the correct conclusion are the figure and the type of premise. Which premise is possible or necessary rather than assertoric? Are the premises universal or particular, and are they affirmative or negative? The *Prior Analytics* i.13 -22 explores

90. *Ibid.*, i.24.41^{b}5 -6.
91. *Ibid.*, i.24.41^{b}7 -9.
92. *Post. An.* ii.3.90^{b}6.
93. *Ibid.*, ii.3.90^{b}6.
94. *Pr. An.* i.12.32 ^{a}6 -9.
95. i.9.30^{a}15 -25.
96. i.9.30^{a}34 -37.
97. i.10.30^{b}7 -9; 31^{a}1 -5.
98. i.11.31^{a}18 -20; 31^{b}10 -15.
99. i.11.31^{a}34 -38; 31^{b}33 -35.

various combinations of these factors and indicates whether a given combination results in no valid conclusion, a possibility, or an assertion. Four examples of the many rules in these chapters give the flavor of this section:

6a. "In the second figure whenever both premisses are problematic, no syllogism is possible. . . . But when one premiss is assertoric, the other problematic, if the affirmative is assertoric no syllogism is possible, but if the universal negative is assertoric a conclusion can always be drawn. Similarly when one premiss is necessary, the other problematic."[100]

6b. In the second figure "Whenever the affirmative proposition is assertoric, whether universal or particular, no syllogism is possible. . . ., but when the negative proposition is assertoric, a conclusion can be drawn by means of conversion."[101]

6c. In the third figure "If one premiss is pure, the other problematic, the conclusion will be problematic."[102]

6d. In the third figure "If one of the premisses is necessary, the other problematic, when the premisses are affirmative a problematic affirmative conclusion can always be drawn; when one proposition is affirmative, the other negative, if the affirmative is necessary a problematic negative can be inferred; but if the negative proposition is necessary both a problematic and a pure negative conclusion are possible. But a necessary negative conclusion will not be possible.[103]

7. If the conclusion is to be essential, the middle must be essential. ". . .a conclusion containing essential nature must be inferred through a middle which is an essential nature."[104]

8. A necessary middle term, which is indispensable to demonstration, insures a necessary conclusion. Otherwise, the nature of the conclusion cannot be foretold. ". . .demonstrative

100. i.17.36^{b}26 -33.
101. i.18.37^{b}39 -38^{a}4.
102. i.21.39^{b}8 -9.
103. i.22.40^{a}4 -10.
104. *Post. An.* ii.8.93^{a}10 -11.

knowledge. . . must clearly be obtained through a necessary middle term; otherwise its possessor will know neither the cause nor the fact that his conclusion is a necessary connexion."[105]

Conversion and *Reductio.ad Impossible*

Such rules, when mastered, must have saved dialecticians and other reasoners a great deal of time in handling deductive materials. Similarly, a full understanding of conversion must have been valuable. Briefly, when a valid interchange of the subject and the predicate in a premise would create a form more suitable for further examination than the original, Aristotle used conversion. By this device he transformed syllogisms from the second and the third figures to the first.[106] The reasoner, of course, needs instruction in how to make valid conversions and in knowing which conversions will be helpful.   The placing of the basic treatment of conversion near the beginning of the *Prior Analytics* (chs. 2 and 3) may indicate the importance of this device to syllogistic manipulation. The rules for the four possible types of assertoric premises are not difficult, but they also are not in all instances self-evident:[107]

Type of Premise	Original Statement	Conversion
Universal negative	No A is B	No B is A
Universal affirmative	Every A is B	Some B is A
Particular affirmative	Some A is B	Some B is A
Particular negative	(Conversion is not possible.)	

---

105. *Ibid.,* i.6.75^{a}12 -14.

106. ". . .the syllogisms in these figures are made perfect by means of universal syllogisms in the first figure and are reduced to them. That every syllogism without qualification can be so treated will be clear presently." *Pr. An.* i.23.40^{b}17 -21. See also *ibid.,* i.7.29^{b}1-2.

107. ". . .in universal attribution the terms of the negative premiss should be convertible, e.g. if no pleasure is good, then no good will be pleasure; the terms of the affirmative must be convertible, not however universally, but in part, e.g. if every pleasure is good, some good must be pleasure; the particular affirmative must convert in part (for if some pleasure is good, then some good will be pleasure); but the particular negative need not convert." *Ibid.,* i.2.25^a 6 -12.

The same rules apply when premises are necessary,[108] and for affirmatives when premises are contingent.[109]

Another manipulative device, besides conversion, is *reductio ad impossible,* which is a form of indirect proof. The reasoner assumes the contradictory of a premise and the impossibility of the conclusion that follows from it. Since the conclusion is false, the premise must be false; and if the premise is false, then the premise of which it is' the contradictory must be true. The procedure, like direct (or ostensive) proof, can be used in all three figures,[110] and Aristotle employs it frequently in his own logical demonstrations.[111] The rules, in general, are the same as for direct proof.[112] Aristotle states that affirmative proof is the preferred method, negative second, and *reductio ad impossible* third,[113] and he gives particular attention to the danger of introducing a false cause during reduction.[114] The basis for deciding whether to use the device is that "When the falsity of the conclusion is the better known, we use *reductio ad impossible;* when the major premiss of the syllogism is the more obvious, we use direct demonstration."[115]

The following passage is a succinct explanation:

Demonstration *per impossibile* differs from ostensive proof in that it posits what it wishes to refute by reduction to a statement admitted to be false; whereas ostensive proof starts from admitted positions. Both, indeed, take two premisses that are admitted, but the latter takes the

108. The following are the rules when premises are necessary: "The universal negative converts universally; each of the affirmatives converts into a particular.... But the particular negative does not convert."*Ibid.,* i.3. 25 ^{a}28 -35.

109. "...affirmative statements will all convert in a manner similar to those described.... But in negative statements the case is different ....the universal negative premiss does not convert, and the particular does." *Ibid.,* i.3.25^{a}39 -25^{b}18.

110. *Ibid.,* ii.11.61^{a}20; ^{a}34 -35.

111. Troy Organ records almost a dozen such instances in his *Index,* and this figure probably is an underestimation. *Index to Aristotle* (Princeton, N.J.: Princeton University Press, 1949), p. 139.

112. *Pr. An.* ii.14.63^{a}12 -21.

113. *Post. An.* i.26.87^{a}28 -30.

114. *Pr. An.* ii.17.65^{a}40 -65^{b}13; *Soph. Ref.* Ch. 5. 167^{b}23 -35.

115. *Post. An.* i.26.87^{a}14 -16.

premisses from which the syllogism starts, the former takes one of these, along with the contradictory of the original conclusion. Also in the ostensive proof it is not necessary that the conclusion should be known, nor that one should suppose beforehand that it is true or not: in the other it is necessary to suppose beforehand that it is not true. It makes no difference whether the conclusion is affirmative or negative; the method is the same in both cases. Everything which is concluded ostensively can be proved *per impossibile,* and that which is proved *per impossibile* can be proved ostensively, through the same terms.[116]

CAUSATION AS A FOUNDATION OF DEMONSTRATION

Finally, any introductory chapter on Aristotle's system of deduction must deal with causation, which he developed far beyond the level of his predecessors. The importance to both the logical and the philosophical systems is beyond question. Not only does Aristotle flatly assert that causation is a significant element, but also the amount of space given in the *Posterior Analytics,* the *Physics,* and the *Metaphysics* stands as evidence. Negatively, the almost total absence of causation from the *Rhetoric,* the *Poetics,* the *Topics,* and the *Prior Analytics* indicates with precision just where Aristotle placed cause within his total writings. It is worthwhile to note that causation is an essential part of the attempted explanation of the natural world and of metaphysical Being,[117] that it adds a significant dimension to that portion of the deductive system whose concern is scientific truth, and that it is relatively unimportant elsewhere.

But why did Aristotle make cause a major feature of demonstration and neglect it in dialectic and rhetoric? The reason is that the need for it was acute in the former but not in the non-sciences. In the first place, since truth was the only objective of demonstration, every possible step was to be taken to lead to an absolute outcome; on the other hand, the natures of rhetoric and

116. *Pr. An.* ii.14.62^{b}29 -40. See also *Post. An.* i.26.87^{a}1 -11.

117. G. R. G. Mure describes causation as "the foundation of Aristotle's theory of knowledge." *Aristotle* (New York: Oxford University Press, 1932), p. 13. Also: "Yet the fourfold causal analysis is the permanent centre of his philosophy and the crucial test to which he brings the metaphysic of his predecessors." *Ibid.,* p. 15.

dialectic imposed no comparable urgencies. Truth was subsidiary in rhetoric, whose primary material was the premise that the listener accepted or created, and in dialectic, whose premise was the choice made by the respondent. In the second place, demonstration needed causation as a corrective to overemphasis on abstract theorizing, whereas this danger was relatively unimportant to rhetoric and dialectic. Rhetoric, in particular, was very much in touch with the "real world," and no speaker was likely to overlook observable events as a part of the means of proof. In the case of demonstration, however, the elaborate analysis of formal features created the risk that the importance of actual correctness would be overlooked. Indeed, inadequately informed critics and would-be disciples have made that mistake repeatedly.

The great contribution of causation to deduction, thus, was its addition of nonformal dimensions that provided a means of relating the reasoning process to reality. As for formal rigor and correctness, causation in Aristotle was of slight importance and was largely redundant; the detailed analysis of structure was sufficient to insure proper relations among terms and premises in the abstract. The dangers were that the syllogizing might start at some point that was not true in actuality and that those engaged in scientific thought might become so concerned with reasoning as such that they would fail to engage in a purposeful examination of the real world. Man, Aristotle said, should be satisfied with nothing less than a deep and thorough understanding.[118]

Briefly and basically, therefore, demonstration sought conclusions that were correct factually as well as formally and that were a product of understanding as well as logical manipulation. The inclusion of causation was the principal means of making these additions to the structural treatment. Completely viewed, demonstration requires both formal validity *and* correct causal relationship, it depends on first principles *and* causation,[119] and the middle term is the cause as well as the link connecting the two

---

118. "...to have reasoned knowledge of a conclusion is to know it through its cause. We may conclude that the middle must be consequentially connected with the minor, and the major with the middle." *Post. An.* i.6.75^{a}34 -37. See also *ibid.,* ii.2.90^{a}31; *Phys.* ii.3.194^{b}19 -21.

119. *Meta.* i.2.982^{b}2 -3. *On the Soul* iii.5.430^{a}9 -13. The translation is by J. A. Smith.

premises. "In any case of conflict between theory and empirical data," states Richard McKeon, "formal preconceptions must be abandoned in favor of adherence to facts."[120]

Aristotle's Contribution

Providing factual accuracy and true wisdom, therefore, is the first and the most important of the contributions that result from the analysis of causation. In Aristotle's own estimation the value was great. "Clearly then Wisdom is knowledge about certain principles and causes," he states in the *Metaphysics*;[121] and in the *Posterior Analytics* he makes knowledge of the cause a factor distinguishing the scientist from the sophist:

> We suppose ourselves to possess unqualified scientific knowledge of a thing, as opposed to knowing it in the accidental way in which the sophist knows, when we think that we know the cause on which the fact depends, as the cause of the fact and of no other, and further, that the fact could not be other than it is.[122]

That this contribution was indeed Aristotle's becomes clear when one compares his treatment of cause with that of his predecessors. Theories of scientific method generally had been seriously incomplete and erroneous,[123] and in respect to causation specifically Aristotle justly charged earlier scholars with two broad deficiencies. None of them had identified all four causes, and none had attained a clear and complete theory.[124] Aristotle largely remedied both shortcomings: (1) He developed the theory of all four causes and particularly that for the efficient and the

120. "Aristotle's Conception of the Development and the Nature of Scientific Method," *Journal of the History of Ideas,* VIII (Jan., 1947), 39.

121. i.1.982^{a}1 -2. Similar statements appear in a number of places, including *ibid.,* i.1.981^{a}14 -^{b}13 and i.3. 983^{a}23 -25.

122. i.2.71^{b}8 -11.

123. See McKeon, esp. pp. 3-34. See also *Phys.* esp. i.1-4, ii.3, and iii.4-5; and *Meta.* esp. i.3-9.

124. "It is evident. . . that all men seek the causes named in the *Physics* (ii.3 and ii.7), and that we cannot name any beyond these; but they seek these vaguely; and though in a sense they have all been described before, in a sense they have not been described at all." *Meta.* i.10. 993 ^{a}10 -15. See also i.7.988^{a}22 -23.

final, and (2) he brought the analyses of the four together in a single place.

The names given the four causes vary slightly from one work to another, and the treatment varies according to the distinctive nature of the volume in which it appears.[125] Perhaps the clearest single description of the causes that commonly bear the respective names *material, formal, efficient,* and *final* is the one in the *Physics:*

> In one sense, then, (1) that out of which a thing comes to be and which persists, is called "cause", e.g. the bronze of the statue, the silver of the bowl, and the genera of which the bronze and the silver are species.
>
> In another sense (2) the form or the archetype, i.e. the statement of the essence, and its genera, are called "cause" . . . .
>
> Again (3) the primary source of the change or coming to rest; e.g. the man who gave advice is a cause, the father is cause of the child, and generally what makes of what is made and what causes change of what is changed.
>
> Again (4) in the sense of end or "that for the sake of which" a thing is done, e.g. health is the cause of walking about. ("Why is he walking about?" we say. "To be healthy", and, having said that, we think we have assigned the cause.)[126]

Still other theoretical contributions are numerous. Aristotle relates causation to actuality and potentiality,[127] and he distinguishes between true causation and change and spontaneity, which he calls incidental causes and says are not necessarily related to conclusions.[128] "Generic effects," he points out, "should be assigned to generic causes, particular effects to particular causes."[129] Several types of causes, he states, may apply in the same instance.[130]

---

125. Cf. the following passage from the *Physics* with *Meta.* i.3.983[a]25 -[b]1, *Post. An.* ii.11.94[a]21 -23 and *On the Soul* ii.4.415[b]8 -11.

126. ii.3.194[b]23 -34. Cf. *Meta.* i.3.983[a]26 -33 and v.1.1013[a]24 -[b]3; *Post. An.* ii.16.94[a]21 -23.

127. *Phys.* ii.3.195[b] 4 -30

128. *Ibid.,* ii.4, 5.

129. *Ibid.,* ii.3.195[b]25 -26.

130. "As the word has several senses, it follows that there are several causes of the same thing. . ., e.g. both the art of the sculptor and the bronze are causes of the statue." *Ibid.,* ii.3.195[a]2 -5.

The advice bearing specifically on demonstration, of course, appears in the *Posterior Analytics,* and here the detail is great. Among the problems to which Aristotle gives his attention are plurality of cause (ii.16), whether different causes may produce the same effect (ii.17; also *Metaphysics* xii.4), the relation of time to cause and effect (ii.12; also *Metaphysics* xii.3), a chain of causes (i.2 and ii.18), whether cause is internal or external (ii.8 and ii.9), and the relation of cause to the middle term (ii.11 and ii.15).

Summary

Aristotle's concepts of the connection of things are of slight importance to dialectic and rhetoric, but they form a critical part of the system of deduction for scientific purposes. This inclusion of causation is further evidence of the rigiorous tests that demonstration must meet in order to be valid. Whereas formal correctness is the objective in dialectic and credibility the test of rhetoric, in science, where the aim is truth, a conclusion must meet two tests — that of structural correctness and that of valid cause-effect relation.

So, as a second dimension of demonstration, causation is vital to Aristotle's system of deduction. The middle term is cause, and the conclusion effect; otherwise, the necessity of the conclusion is not certain. Only those who know the cause possess scientific knowledge.[131] The bases of Aristotle's system of deduction, to repeat, are two: first principles and causes.

CONCLUSION

The purposes of this chapter have been to supply a working vocabulary and to present in a simple form such notions basic to Aristotelian deduction as terms, premises, predication, categories, figures, modes, the laws of thought, contraries, contradictories, conversion, and cause. Much of this introduction is applicable to the study of deduction at all levels; for, although science, rhetoric, and dialectic differ in purpose, environment, rigor, and the substance of premises, they follow the same rules for formal validity.[132]

131. *Post. An.* ii.11.94^{a}20 -21.
132. *Pr. An.* ii.23.68^{b}10-14.

The importance of logic to Aristotle's system of knowledge is beyond question. The mechanism for scientific thought is logic, dialectic discourse is applied logic, and in rhetoric the ultimate means of persuasion, though pathos and ethos may have telling effects upon receptiveness, is the enthymeme. Moreover, only through thought can one construct a message and analyze an audience, whether he be ancient Greek or modern man. Proof that Aristotle realized the importance of logic to discourse lies both in explicit statements and in the implication to be found in the amount of attention he gave to the subject.

". . . it was Aristotle who first constituted logic as a separate science, and it was Aristotle who discovered, isolated and analyzed the fundamental form of inference, namely, the syllogism."[133] Richard McKeon in characterizing Aristotle's scientific method, which was one aspect of the total system of deduction, states, "Its novelties center about the treatment of causes, by which the application of principles to things is insured, and the analysis of terms and propositions, by which the accuracy of statement and inference is ascertained."[134] John H. Randall writes similarly of fundamental truths and causes as the bases of science.[135] Aristotle himself wrote, ". . . all men suppose what is called Wisdom to deal with the first causes and the principles of things . . . . Clearly . . . Wisdom is knowledge about certain principles and causes."[136]

133. Frederick Copleston, *A History of Philosophy,* Vol. I (Garden City, N. Y.: Image Books, 1962), 26 -27.

134. *Introduction to Aristotle* (New York: Modern Library, 1947), p. xiv. See also pp. 3 -4.

135. ". . . we have a genuine 'science,' *episteme,* when we can state in precise language not only that things are so, *hoti,* but also *why* they are as they are, *dioti,* and why they have to be that way. . . . 'Science' . . .is a knowledge of the dependence of true statement on more fundamental truths, on 'first things,' *ta prota,* or 'causes,' *aitia.*" Pp. 33 -34.

136. *Meta.* i.1.981^{b}26 -982^{a}2.

CHAPTER 3

THE PREMISES AND THE MATERIALS OF DEDUCTION

Chapter 2 was an examination of several major structural features of Aristotle's deductive system. The general topic now shifts to substance and materials. What kinds of question does Aristotle deem appropriate for deductive thought in the sciences and the nonsciences respectively? What is the nature of premises, and what are their sources? How does the process of definition relate to the content of premises, and how do formal requirements affect content? Answers to these questions necessitate a close examination of several different works in the corpus and a considerable amount of analysis and reorganization.

One problem that arises is that a person must write about one element of the system at a time even though the parts are interrelated. Structure and content, for example, are not strictly separable, as both chapters 2 and 3 should clearly indicate. The most that a writer can hope for is that he will focus upon separate elements enough to be lucid and that he will bring in related factors sufficiently to be reasonably accurate.

The interconnected nature of the elements of the system also deserves attention because the failure to note this feature misleads some critics. Those who say that Aristotle's deduction is rigid and unrealistic overlook the fact that the total system includes materials on deductive thought in dialectic and rhetoric as well as in science. When all parts are viewed collectively, the system is broad and flexible. The product of both common sense and theoretic analysis, the system when properly understood is well adapted to most situations that face the deductive reasoner.

QUALITIES OF BOTH SCIENTIFIC AND NONSCIENTIFIC PREMISES

Structurally, as pointed out in the preceding chapter, syllogisms are the same in all environments. At both the scientific and the nonscientific level, to review, a syllogism consists of two premises, each of which is composed of a subject, a predicate, and a connecting verb that expresses an affirmation or a denial of the relation between the two. Moreover, if the reasoning is to be clear, if unambiguous communication is to occur, the terms must be univocal and the predication careful. "A proposition," Aristotle states, "predicates a single attribute of a single subject."[1] Finally, the construction of a premise through predication always involves an accident, a genus, a property, or a definition.

These similarities, of course, are in structure and in the mechanism of predication. In substance, on the other hand, only one likeness is plain. In all syllogisms, whether scientific or non-scientific, "All instruction given or received by way of argument proceeds from pre-existent knowledge."[2] The lines that follow make the meaning of "all" unmistakable; and although the *Posterior Analytics* for the most part is restricted to demonstration, this passage continues by stating that this observation is also applicable to dialectic and rhetoric. "The mathematical science and all other speculative disciplines are acquired in this way, and so are the two forms of dialectical reasoning, syllogistic and inductive . . . . Again the persuasion exerted by rhetorical arguments is in principle the same."[3]

In regard to materials, a section on features common to all three areas of syllogistic reasoning, therefore, is very short. The following sections of this chapter are separate treatments of demonstrative and nonscientific premises.

DEMONSTRATIVE PREMISES

An examination of the nature of demonstrative premises is also an examination of the nature of demonstration; and since the distinctions among the scientific, the dialectic and the rhetorical syllogisms are in the content of the premises rather than in their formal qualities, the sections that follow constitute an analysis of the major characteristics that distinguish among the three. *Syllogism*, it should be noted, is a broad term and *demonstration* a

1. *Posterior Analytics* i.2.72^{a}8 -9. The translation is by G. R. G.Mure.
2. *Ibid.*, i.2.71^{a}1 -2.
3. i.2.71^{a}3 -9.

narrow one: "Syllogism should be discussed before demonstration, because syllogism is the more general: the demonstration is a sort of syllogism but not every syllogism is a demonstration."[4]

The nature of the content of the demonstrative premise is not an easy topic, and only by examining several types of material is an adequate analysis possible. The writer's method is to move from general descriptions of the substance of demonstration to materials that bear on specific wordings.

Questions of Scientific Concern

First, what kinds of questions form the subject matter of demonstration? Aristotle's answer, which appears in the opening section of Book ii of the *Posterior Analytics,* is a list of four topics for inquiry: "(1) whether the connexion of an attribute with a thing is a fact, (2) what is the reason of the connexion, (3) whether a thing exists, (4) what is the nature of the thing."[5] "Under the first head," George Grote explains, "come questions of Fact; under the second head, questions of Cause or Reason; under the third, questions of Existence; under the fourth, questions of Essence."[6]

An analysis of these four heads, whose Latin names are *quod, cur, an sit,* and *quod sit,* shows that they really are two pairs with the second and the fourth becoming meaningful only if the answers to the first and the third respectively are affirmative. Aristotle points out that "when we know the fact we ask the reason"[7] and that "when we have ascertained the thing's existence, we inquire as to its nature."[8] In other words, the two fundamental subjects for demonstrative thought are "Is ———— a fact? " and "Does ———— exist? " and the two secondary subjects are those of reason and essence. "These, then, are the four kinds of question we ask, and it is in the answers to these questions that our knowledge consists."[9]

4. *Prior Analytics* i.4.25^{b}28 -31. The translation is by A. J. Jenkinson.

5. ii.1.89^{b}23 -25.

6. *Aristotle*, ed. Alexander Bain and G. C. Robertson (London, 1883), p. 238.

7. *Post. An.* ii.1.89^{b}29.

8. *Ibid.,* ii.1.89^{b}34.

9. *Ibid.,* ii.2.89^{b}35 -36.

So far as subject matter is concerned, the foregoing statements identify the distinctive nature of demonstration. Just as the distinctive character of the formal features is certainty, so is it with substance. Whether something is a fact and whether something exists are questions admitting of incontestible answers regardless of whether the approach is empirical or through a chain of syllogisms. The contrast between these subjects and those characteristic of dialectic and rhetoric is plain. The materials of dialectic are opinions, and the principal questions to which the rhetorician responds are matters far from certain. "Is it expedient? " is the principal topic for deliberative oratory; "Is it just? " for forensic, and "Is it praiseworthy? " for epideictic. To each of these questions only a probable answer is possible.

Subject Matter of Premises

The next step in the present inquiry is to determine the kinds of materials that the reasoner employs in his study of the two general topics — factuality and existence — and the two secondary topics — cause and essence. The number of kinds is twofold. The first of these is ideas, both universal and particular,[10] coming from the science with which the reasoner is dealing. These materials, secured through perception, intuition, and prosyllogisms, consist of the primary premise for the science, premises derived from the primary, and materials secured through investigation and intuitive thought. Each of these items must be true and certain. The scope is wide in many respects, but the materials, with only a few exceptions, are restricted by the rule that they must come from the single genus, which is the science. One cannot prove a conclusion in geometry through premises that are arithmetical, Aristotle says, and one cannot prove that a straight line is the

10. Cf. "With respect to the subject matter of science, therefore, Aristotle's investigations of science and method lead him to the recognition that science must in some sense treat of changing phenomena and also to the conclusion that it must state a changeless truth." Richard McKeon, "Aristotle's Conception of the Development and the Nature of Scientific Method," *Journal of the History of Ideas*, VIII (Jan., 1947), p. 20.

most beautiful of lines through premises whose genus is geometry.[11]

The only commonly used type of premise that does not need to belong to the particular genus is the axiom.[12] The development of this point is brief and not entirely clear, but the example "Take equals from equals and equals remain,"[13] as well as the general nature of the explanation, indicates that Aristotle had in mind generally accepted and largely self-evident truths that were applicable to many situations. In fact, he states, "The axioms which are premisses of demonstration may be identical in two or more sciences."[14] Axioms alone, however, cannot form demonstrations; proof is possible only when at least one premise arises out of the subject matter of the science.[15]

Definition as a Factor in Premises

To state an axiom or a premise substantive to the particular science, however, may leave the actual content uncertain. The true substance, as Aristotle clearly understood, is not the words as such but the ideas that the words represent. Correct definition, as a consequence, is indispensable to proper demonstration.

The functions of definition and demonstration, however, are distinct. By defining, one does not prove or demonstrate, Aristotle insists, and in the usual and strict sense one does not define through demonstration.[16] Definition, nevertheless, is so

11. *Post. An.* i.7. The entire chapter deals with this requirement. See also *ibid.*, i.24.84^{b}18 -19 and i.28.87^{a}37 -^{b}4.

12. ". . .there are three elements in demonstration: (1) what is proved, the conclusion – an attribute inhering essentially in a genus; (2) the axioms, i.e. axioms which are premisses of demonstration; (3) the subject-genus whose attributes, i.e. essential properties, are revealed by the demonstration." *Post. An.* i.7.74^{a}40 -^{b}3. See also *ibid.*, i.10.76^{b}12 -16.

13. *Ibid.*, i.10.76^{b}20.

14. *Ibid.*, i.7.75^{b}2 -3. For a detailed development of the position that axioms do not belong to a single science, see the *Metaphysics* iii.2.996^b 26 -997^{a}14 and iv.3.1005^{a}18 -^{b}34. From this position it follows that the study of axioms cannot belong to any special science but is within the province of metaphysics.

15. *Post. An.* i.32.88^{b}2 -4.

16. *Ibid.*, ii.3 *et passim.*

crucial to the process of demonstration that about half of Book ii
of the *Posterior Analytics* and Book vi and part of Book vii of the
Topics are on defining. Definition also occupies a prominent place
in the *Metaphysics*. On the other hand, in the *Rhetoric* and the
Poetics emphasis shifts from definition to style. The reason seems
clear: these forms of communication are concerned with producing effects rather than with precision of thought.

But what does Aristotle say about definition that is relevant
to the present purpose? His principal point is that only through
definition can the meaning of a statement be made clear. To
achieve clarity, the reasoner must define in ways appropriate to
the nature of the term. The goal when defining an attribute or an
event is to state the cause,[17] but the more common and more
crucial task is that of defining through a phrase signifying essence.[18] Consistent with the foremost place accorded substance in
the *Categories* is the treatment in the *Metaphysics*. A definition of
a term, Aristotle says, must include a definition of its substance.[19]
"And we think we know each thing most fully when we know
what it is, e.g. what man is or what fire is, rather than when we
know its quality, its quantity, or its place; since we know each of
these predicates also, only when we know *what* the quantity or
the quality *is.*"[20]

How one creates definitions receives detailed attention.
Ultimately they are the products of perspicuous thought,[21] but
induction and quasi-demonstration sometimes are helpful. In ii.13
of the *Posterior Analytics* Aristotle describes how one can proceed
from observations of sets of particulars to "a single formula,"[22]
and in ii.10 he illustrates a quasi-demonstration whose purpose is
arriving at a definition,[23] though not demonstrating it.

As for the mechanism of definition, the Aristotelian system

17. *Ibid.,* ii.10.93^{b}28 -94^{a}10.

18. Aristotle makes this point consistently and repeatedly. For example,
see *Post. An.* ii.3.91^{a}1 and ii.10.93^{b}28 and the *Topics* i.4.101^{b}21 and
i.5.101^{b}38 -102^{a}1.

19. *Meta.* vii.1.1028^{a}35. The translation is by W. D. Ross.

20. *Ibid.,* vii.1.1028^{a}37 -^{b}2.

21. *Post. An.* ii.13.97^{b}31.

22. 97^{b}6 -37. See also *Top.* i.18.108^{b}19 -28.

23. 94^{a}1-10.

of placing the term within its genus and appending differentiae[24] is well known. Not so familiar to modern readers, though, is the advice to move by successive stages to the final indivisible level.[25] The major points to observe in carrying out this process, according to Aristotle's summary, are "(1) the admission only of elements in the definable form, (2) the arrangement of these in the right order, (3) the omission of no such elements."[26] In the finished statement of the definition, however, only the genus and the final differentiae should appear.[27]

Elsewhere Aristotle states that a definition must always be a phrase and not a term[28] and that one should continue to define terms appearing in a succession of definitions until nothing ambiguous remains.[29] Still further advice on defining may be inferred from the commonplace rules governing predications of definition. The sections on the avoidance of obscurity and redundancy[30] and on the need for using terms that are prior and more intelligible[31] are especially relevant to one's needs when defining.

In summary, definition has an important bearing on the nature of the demonstrative premise, and Aristotle gives the nature and the process of definition careful attention. He also is careful to avoid any confusion of the roles of definition and demonstration.

Formal Requirements with Implications for Content

Finally, to answer the question on the nature of the demon-

24. Aristotle writes so casually about this that it seems that he takes familiarity with this mechanism for granted. For example, see *Top.* vi.1. 139^a27 -32 and vii.3.153^b13 -15.

25. *Post. An.* ii.13. See also *Meta.* vii.12.1037^b28-1038^a35.

26. *Post. An.* ii.13.97^a23 -25.

27. *Meta.* vii.12.1037^b29 -1038^a4.

28. *Top.* i.5.102^a2 -5. The translation is by W. A. Pickard-Cambridge.

29. "A man should substitute definitions also for the terms contained in his definitions, and stop until he comes to a familiar term: for often if the definition be rendered whole, the point at issue is not cleared up, whereas if for one of the terms used in the definition a definition be stated, it becomes obvious." *Ibid.*, ii.2.110^a4 -9.

30. *Ibid.*, vi.1 -3.

31. *Ibid.*, vi.4.

strative premise the scholar must examine the principal features of the scientific system. A passage near the beginning of the *Posterior Analytics* suggests an organization for the present section: "... the premisses of demonstrated knowledge must be true, primary, immediate, better known than and prior to the conclusion, which is further related to them as effect to cause."[32]

True, Necessary, Essential, and Commensurately Universal

Aristotle, as the preceding chapter indicates, combined a common sense empiricism with theoretic analysis in dealing with premises. It is not surprising, therefore, that in demonstration he required premises to be true in the sense that they be consistent with observation and good judgment. Truth in this sense, however, was not a sufficient basis for demonstrative thought, nor was it even the characteristic and foremost test. "For though you may reason from true premises without demonstrating, yet if your premises are necessary you will assuredly demonstrate: in such necessity you have at once a distinctive character of demonstration."[33]

But the relation of necessity to demonstration goes beyond distinctiveness; indispensability is an accurate term. "... since demonstrative knowledge is only present when we have a demonstration, it follows that demonstration is an inference from necessary premisses."[34] The reason for this indispensable relation is plain: in demonstration one deals only in certainties, and the meaning of *necessity* in this context is "true in every instance." "... for this is what 'being necessary' means — that it is impossible for the thing not to be," Aristotle writes in the *Metaphysics*.[35] Later in the same work the language is somewhat different: "... not necessity in the sense of compulsion but that which we assert of things because they cannot be otherwise."[36] Serving

32. i.2.71^{b}20 -22.

33. *Ibid.*, i.6.74^{b}15 -18. Even more obvious evidence that *truth* and *necessity* are synonymous appears at 75^{a}2 -3: "You can in fact infer the necessary from a non-necessary premiss, just as you can infer the true from the not true."

34. *Ibid.*, i.4.73^{a}33 -34.

35. iv.4.1006^{b}32 -33.

36. vi.2.1026^{b}28 -29. See also xi.8.1064^{b}34 and xii.7. 1072^{b}11-13.

further to clarify and to emphasize the meaning is the statement on the best way to refute a claim that a premise is necessary. This best method, as the reader can guess, is to cite a contrary instance.[37]

So far the present discussion of *necessity* has been in a quantitative sense – that all instances be in accord. In places in the corpus the meaning is broader, and sometimes Aristotle finds it desirable to specify the sense in which he is using the term. In *On Sleep and Waking necessity* refers to the endowments that an animal must have in order to exist,[38] and in the *Metaphysics* at one point Aristotle speaks of three senses in which *necessary* may be used.[39]

Although knowing that variant meanings exist in certain contexts is a safeguard against confusion, it is sufficient in dealing with demonstrative premises to continue to define *necessity* as "true in every instance." For the quality of inevitability, a sense which *necessity* assumes in some uses, the proper term in Aristotle is *essentiality*.

The addition of this characteristic further increases the rigor of pure demonstration. Invariability, Aristotle states in the *Posterior Analytics,* is not always a sufficient basis for reasoned knowledge.[40] The relation of attribute to subject, besides being true and invariable, must be essential. Defined, this means that the relation of attribute to subject must be inevitable as well as invariable. Either the attribute must belong to its subject as an element in the latter's essential nature (as *line* to *triangle,* which is composed of lines) or the subject to which the attribute belongs must be contained in the attribute's own defining formula (as *line* is the subject to which the attribute *curved* belongs, and the formula defining *curved* must include the subject *line*).[41] The

37. *Post. An.* i.4.73^{a}32 -34.
38. Ch. 2.455^{b}25 -27.
39. xii.7.1072^{b}10 -13.
40. ". . .since accidents are not necessary one does not necessarily have reasoned knowledge of a conclusion drawn from them (this is so even if the accidental premisses are invariable but not essential)." i.6.75 ^{a}32 -33.
41. *Ibid.,* i.4.73^{a}34 -^{b}2. Aristotle adds two other situations in which attributes are essentially related to their subjects (73^{b}5 -15), but the two cited here are the ones vital to a characterizing of science.

relation of predicate to subject, in other words, is *per se,* not merely *de omni* as in necessity. In contrast to essential is accidental, and clearly a premise in which the relation of predicate to subject is an accident cannot lead to a demonstration.

Aristotle's explanation of essentiality does not go much beyond the passages and the ideas already cited, but the language of the translators is clearer in some instances than in others. ". . . all attributes which are essential either in the sense that their subjects are contained in them, or in the sense that they are contained in their subjects, are necessary as well as consequentially connected with their subjects"[42] is one such passage, and another occurs in i.22 of the *Posterior Analytics.* "Now attributes may be essential for two reasons: either because they are elements in the essential nature of their subjects, or because their subjects are elements in their essential nature."[43] As contrasted with necessity, essentiality is determined abstractly and formally rather than empirically.

At the ultimate level in this sequence of qualities of the demonstrative premise is the commensurately universal:

> I term "commensurately universal" an attribute which belongs to every instance of its subject, and to every instance essentially and as such; from which it clearly follows that all commensurate universals inhere *necessarily* in their subjects. The essential attribute, and the attribute that belongs to its subject as such, are identical.[44]

Aristotle follows this definition by pointing to a test[45] and by explaining in a detailed example how to determine which is the first thing to which an attribute may belong.[46] In the succeeding chapters he deals with some mistakes that often occur in the commensurately universal.

Here in the commensurately universal deduction attains its

---

42. *Ibid.,* i.4.73[b]16 -18.

43. 84[a]12 -13.

44. *Ibid.,* i.4.73[b]26 -29.

45. "An attribute belongs commensurately and universally to a subject when it can be shown to belong to any random instance of that subject and when the subject is the first thing to which it can be shown to belong." i.4.73[b]31 -33.

46. i.4.73[b]33 -74[a]1.

purest form. Such proof deals only with eternals (or nonperisha-
bles)[47] and with abstractions:

> ...that which is commensurately universal and true in all cases one
> cannot perceive, since it is not 'this' and it is not 'now.' [The term
> *commensurately universal* is the one] we apply to what is always and
> everywhere. Seeing, therefore, that demonstrations are commensurate-
> ly universal and universals imperceptible, we clearly cannot obtain
> scientific knowledge by the act of perception. ... perception must be
> of a particular, whereas scientific knowledge involves the recognition of
> the commensurate universal.[48]

In summary, this first set of requirements for demonstration
moves through ascending degrees of rigor from true through necessary and essential to commensurately universal. The restrictions
upon the relation of subject and predicate, and hence upon the
nature of the scientifically acceptable premise, are severe.

Primary or Immediate

A second requirement for the subject matter of demonstration is that the syllogism if traced back must rest on the "basic
truth" for the particular science. Quoted earlier is the passage
including "primary" among the requirements, and a few lines later
Aristotle explains what he means:

> In saying that the premisses of demonstrated knowledge must be
> primary, I mean that they must be the "appropriate" basic truths, for I
> identify primary premiss and basic truth. A "basic truth" in a demon-
> stration is an immediate proposition. An immediate proposition is one
> which has no other proposition prior to it.[49]

Numerous restatements and elaborations appear, but nowhere is

---

47. "...if the premises from which the syllogism proceeds are commensurately universal, the conclusion... must also be eternal. Therefore no
attribute can be demonstrated nor known by strictly scientific knowledge to
inhere in perishable things. The proof can only be accidental, because the
attribute's connexion with its perishable subject is not commensurately
universal but temporary and special . . . . the conclusion can only be that a
fact is true at the moment — not commensurately and universally." *Ibid.*,
i.8.75^{b}20 -30.
48. *Ibid.*, i.31.87^{b}30 -39.
49. *Ibid.*, i.2.72^{a}5 -8.

Aristotle any plainer: A primary or immediate premise is the basic statement for each of the sciences.

The matter of the primary premise is crucial to Aristotle's system. Unlike Plato and Democritus, who believed in one unified science, Aristotle thought that there were a number of sciences —[50] as many as there were first principles and each with its own first principle. The source of this principle, which in an ultimate sense was basic to all content of demonstration, however, was a problem. Since Aristotle argued that no universal science was prior to the special sciences, there could be no proposition from which the immediate premise of the individual science could be deduced.

But if the immediate premise cannot be located and verified through demonstration, how is it to be found? The answer lies in the observation of particulars and in induction. In the final chapter of the *Posterior Analytics* (ii.19) Aristotle examines the successive stages of sense perception, memory, experience, and "the skill of the craftsman and the knowledge of the man of science" — an approach consistent with the treatment elsewhere of experience and art [51] and with the statements that all knowledge depends on sense perception. ". . .it is consequently impossible to come to grasp universals except through induction," he says. "But induction is impossible for those who have not sense-perception."[52] In *On the Soul* also he speaks of the vital role of sense perception in thought.[53]

This sweeping statement concerning the role of perception seems an exaggeration unless one keeps in mind the precise intellectual operation that Aristotle is explaining. The search is for the first principle of a science. The scholar, Aristotle is saying, should begin with observation, and it is through a storing of the mind with a set of specific instances that the grasping of the first principle becomes possible. Better advice is hard to find, and he does not say that the mind works only during sense perception.

50. McKeon, esp. pp. 16-20.

51. See *Méta.* i.1.

52. *Post. An* i.18.81^{b}5 -6.

53. For example, iii.7.431^{a}16 and iii.8.432^{a}6. Richard McKeon generalizes, "Aristotle was convinced that all knowledge is derived from sensation." *Introduction to Aristotle* (New York: Random House, 1947), p. xv.

But to say that one begins with a series of observations is only a beginning. For a fuller explanation Aristotle's statement — though the introduction of his conception of potentiality-actuality injects a metaphysical note that is strange to the modern reader — still is as reasonable and lucid as any:

> So out of sense-perception comes to be what we call memory, and out of frequently repeated memories of the same thing develops experience; for a number of memories constitute a single experience. From experience again — i.e. from the universal now stabilized in its entirety within the soul, the one beside the many which is a single identity within them all — originate the skill of the craftsman and the knowledge of the man of science.[54]

This account, though directed here to the problem of explaining how one grasps first principles, is a theory of learning broadly applicable. A similar analysis appears in the *Metaphysics* i.l, and a much more detailed treatment is in *On the Soul* ii.6 -12 and iii.3 -8.

In summary,[55] the first principle, which exists in nature, is by definition a premise that is beyond demonstrative proof[56] and from which all of the lesser principles of that one science are derived. The task of man is to use his intellect to find this first principle; the role of sensation is to provide the particulars that stimulate the mind so that it grasps the first principle. Ideally man does this all at once,[57] but more commonly he progresses through intermediate steps. Each of these is a higher level of generalization than the preceding one, and finally apprehension occurs. Here in Aristotle's language is how and why the process succeeds:

> When one of a number of logically indiscrimable particulars has made a stand, the earliest universal is present in the soul; for though the act of sense-perception is of the particular, its content is universal.
> . . .A fresh stand is made among these rudimentary universals, and the

54. *Post. An.* ii.19.100^{a}3 -8.

55. Several scholars give excellent analyses and restatements of the *Posterior Analytics* ii.19. One that is particularly helpful is that by McKeon, *Introduction to Aristotle*, pp. xvi-xvii.

56. Aristotle makes this point repeatedly in the *Posterior Analytics* — e.g., i.3.72^{b}19 -20 and i.10.76^{a}30 -32.

57. "Quick wit is a faculty of hitting upon the middle term instantaneously." *Ibid.*, i.34.89^{b}10.

process does not cease until the indivisible concepts, the true universals are established. . . .

Thus it is clear that we must get to know the primary premisses
by induction; for the method by which even sense-perception implants
the universal is inductive.[58]

Intuition, Aristotle says as he continues, is even more accurate
than scientific knowledge, and demonstration cannot produce a
first principle. ". . .intuition," he concludes, "will be the origina-
tive source of scientific knowledge."[59]

Aristotle's writings elsewhere confirm the preceding analysis. The *Nicomachean Ethics* in a statement on the five methods of
finding truth also takes the position that intuitive grasp is the
method by which the first principle is apprehended. ". . .the wise
man must not only know what follows from the first principles,"
Aristotle writes, "but must also possess truth about the first
principles. Therefore wisdom must be intuitive reason combined
with scientific knowledge."[60] Four chapters later is a similar
statement: ". . .the first terms and the last are objects of intuitive
reason and not of argument, and the intuitive reason which is
presupposed by demonstrations grasps the unchangeable and first
terms."[61]

Aristotle's position is firm and unmistakable – an indispensable characteristic of demonstration is that the premises must be
derived from the primary or immediate truth of that particular
science[62] – and calling upon his general theory of learning and his
doctrine of potentiality he provides an explanation of the process
by which intuition leads to a grasp of the primary premise. The
critical remaining question is, "Is a first premise so formulated
true? " No really satisfactory answer is to be found.

In the *Topics* i.2 Aristotle includes a note on the apprehension of primary premises in his discussion of the purposes of

58. *Ibid.*, ii.19.100^{a}15 -^{b}5.

59. ii.19.100^{b}15 -16.

60. vi.7.1141^{a}16 -18. The translation is by W. D. Ross.

61. 1142^{b}35 -1143^{a}2.

62. ". . .his opinion, if obtained through immediate premises, will be
both of the fact and of the reasoned fact; if not so obtained, of the fact
alone." *Post. An.* i.33.89^{a}21 -23.

dialectic,[63] but even dialectic can supply no final answer. Ultimately the first premise must rest on faith. "Things are 'true' and 'primary' which are believed on the strength not of anything else but of themselves: for in regard to the first principles of science it is improper to ask any further for the why and wherefore of them; each of the first principles should command belief in and by itself."[64]

So the method of grasping first principles, despite the elaborate analysis, does not guarantee correctness, nor can it do so. The requirement that the demonstrative premise be immediate or primary, nevertheless, is an additional source of rigor. The scientific reasoner, at least during the time that he employs demonstration either to prove a doctrine or to deduce new knowledge, cannot move freely and speculatively. If he does not work directly with the first principle of the science, he must employ premises derived from it and within the genus.[65]

Better Known and Prior

Aristotle's third requirement, which is related to the second and the fourth, pertains to the position that the premise occupies on the continuum extending from the greatest particularity to the highest universality — the latter, of course, being the first principle for the given science. In other words, this third feature indispensable to demonstration requires that the direction of movement from premise to conclusion be from a position formally close to the first principle to one more distant.

Aristotle's only major concern in his brief exposition of this

---

63. 101^a27-$^b4$. E. M. Cope regards this passage as one which gives a true picture of Aristotle's position: "As the first principles of any special science cannot be demonstrated by the science itself, these, if they are to be investigated at all, must be investigated through the medium of the all sifting, all questioning method of dialectics." *An Introduction to Aristotle's Rhetoric* (London: The Macmillan Company, 1867), p. 80.

64. *Top.* i.1.100^a31-$^b21$. Cope comments, ". . .proof must ultimately depend upon something *accepted* as truth; it must rest ultimately on belief — and they [first principles] are apprehended and verified by the highest faculty, intuitive reason." Pp. 71-72.

65. *Post. An.* i.7, i.28, and i.24.84^b18-19.

point is that of making sure that the sense in which he is using *prior* is understood. This concern is well founded, for his writings contain numerous definitions of *prior*.[66] Here, though, his meaning rests upon the following distinction:

> Now "prior" and "better known" are ambiguous terms, for there is a difference between what is prior and better known in the order of being and what is prior and better known to man. I mean that objects nearer to sense are prior and better known to man; objects without qualification prior and better known are those further from sense. Now the most universal causes are furthest from sense and particular causes are nearest to sense, and they are thus exactly opposed to one another.[67]

"Prior and better known to nature" is the quality required of the demonstrative premise.

The quality of being prior, therefore, means closer to the universal than to the particular and closer to the immediate premise than to the particular premise. Aristotle then makes a less technical analysis. He argues on several grounds that man must know the premise better than the conclusion —[68] an analysis that supports the view that one purpose of demonstration is movement toward new knowledge. The reasoner "must not only have a better knowledge of the basic truths and a firmer conviction of them than of the connexion which is being demonstrated.... For indeed the conviction of pure science must be unshakable."[69]

The insertion of this nonformal requirement into a work on the technical aspects of demonstration is a reminder that Aristotle believed that scientific thought must be in accord with reality as well as formally correct. Earlier in this chapter the requirement that premises be true was considered, and scattered through Aristotle's analysis of demonstration as a logical instrument are state-

66. In the *Categories* he explains five senses (Ch. 12.14^{a}26 -^{b}23), in the *Physics* he speaks of priority in three senses (viii. 7.260^{b}15 -261^{a}27), and in the *Metaphysics* he analyzes four meanings (v.11.1018^{b}8 -1019^{a}14), the second of which is the one applicable to premises in demonstration. Another interesting treatment of priority is the distinction between prior in definition and prior in substance. *Meta.* xiii.2.1077^{b}1 -10.

67. *Post. An.* i.2.71^{b}33 -72^{a}5.

68. *Ibid.*, i.2.72^{a}24 -^{b}4.

69. *Ibid.*, i.2.72^{a}37 -^{b}4.

ments of the need for actual accuracy. For example, the *Posterior Analytics* says, ". . .this antecedent knowledge being not our mere understanding of the meaning, but knowledge of the fact as well."[70]

Interesting and important as these points are, the real significance of Aristotle's third requirement is that the movement from premise to conclusion must be from a statement relatively close to the first principle to one that is relatively further removed.

Causally Connected

The fourth of Aristotle's listed requirements for the demonstrative premise not only is related to the demand for priority but also is one of the two indispensable requirements for scientific knowledge (the other being that the "fact" can be nothing other than what it is).[71] Causation thus is vital to Aristotelian deduction, and the only reason for the brevity of the present treatment is the full discussion in Chapter 2.

Here let it be noted that the concern for causality, like the demand for truth as a criterion, is evidence of Aristotle's insistence that demonstration must be consistent with reality as well as logically correct. That premises be true, necessary, essential, commensurately universal, primary, and prior and better known is not quite enough; to insure further the certainty of the conclusion, as well as to give an understanding of why the conclusion is true, the reasoner is to select premises that are causes of the conclusion.

Other Formal Qualities Affecting Content

A review of some earlier pages now is in order, because some ideas expressed previously bear on the substance of the demonstrative premise. First, thé demand that premises be immediate makes induction and dialectic relevant to the content of

---

70. i.2.71^{b}31 -32. Ch. 13 is a development of the topic sentence "Knowledge of the fact differs from knowledge of the reasoned fact." 78^{a}21 -22.

71. "We suppose ourselves to possess unqualified scientific knowledge of a thing. . . when we think that we know the cause on which the fact depends, as the cause of that fact and of no other, and, further, that the fact could not be other than it is." *Ibid.*, i.2.71^{b}8 -11.

deduction. The reasons are that the source of the immediate premise must be inductive materials and that dialectic is the method for checking the immediate premise. Second, also previously stated, the terms must be univocal — a stipulation that is a prerequisite to logical manipulation but one that also is relevant to the substance of premises. Third, premises must be so chosen that the logical manipulations basic to deduction are possible. The particular must fall within the more general, and both premises, as well as the conclusion, must belong to the same genus.

Also worth noting is Aristotle's preference for the universal premise over the particular. In content, in other words, the more useful premise is the one that states a universal. Aristotle considered the relative merits of universal and particular premises a sufficiently important topic to warrant eight answers to those who favored the latter.[72] The most important reasons of the eight are those in this summary:

> The clearest indication of the precedence of commensurately universal demonstration is as follows: if of two propositions, a prior and a posterior, we have a grasp of the prior, we have a kind of knowledge — a potential grasp — of the posterior as well. . . . but to grasp this posterior proposition is by no means to know the commensurate universal either potentially or actually. Moreover, commensurately universal demonstration is through and through intelligible; particular demonstration issues in sense-perception.[73]

Summary

For an analysis of the nature of demonstrative premises one must examine several types of material. The broad topics appropriate to scientific examination are questions of fact, questions of cause or reason, questions of existence, and questions of essence. Premises dealing with these matters either are axioms or are substantive statements falling within the genus of a particular science. To meet the rigorous requirements of demonstration, these premises must use terms that are properly defined, and they

72. *Ibid.,* i.24.

73. *Ibid.,* i.24.86^{a}21 -30. Grote gives this clear statement: ". . .for he that knows the Universal does in a certain sense know also the Particular; but he that knows the particular cannot be said in any sense to know the Universal." Grote, pp. 232 -233.

must possess the qualities of being true, necessary, essential, and commensurately universal. There must be a basic proposition, and individual premises must be closer to it than to the conclusion. Finally, premises should contain causes, and they should be empirically true as well as conforming to the seemingly theoretical requirements.

NONSCIENTIFIC PREMISES: GENERAL DISCUSSION

Rhetoric and dialectic differ in important respects, but the premises of the two possess some common features that contrast with those of demonstration. These points of difference are not surprising, for in its essential nature and basic purposes science contrasts with these two nonsciences. First, since the two nonsciences are respectively faculties of persuading and of studying noncertainties, they need not conform to the rigid rules that are indispensable to demonstration. The premises of dialectic and rhetoric, true enough, usually entail astuteness and care, but there is no unwavering requirement that they be necessary, essential, commensurately universal, primary, prior, causal, or even true.[74]

Second, the sources of nonscientific premises are almost without limit. Whereas the materials of science are first principles, premises derived deductively from first principles, particulars lieing within the genus, and axioms, the materials of dialectic and rhetoric are whatever premises will enable the reasoner to obtain his objectives. These skills do not have a subject matter of their own -- a quality noted by critics from Plato to the present -- but this is a characteristic that broadens the purview more than it limits. Grote points out the wide range when he writes the following:

> Dialectic and Rhetoric are carefully distinguished by Aristotle from all the special sciences (such as Geometry, Astronomy, Medicine, etc.); and are constructed as embracing every variety of authortitative *dicta*, current beliefs, and matters of opinion, together with all the most general maxims, and hypotheses of Ontology and Metaphysics, of Physics and

74. Negative evidence supplies further support for this conclusion. Whereas Aristotle explicitly discusses these qualities as indispensable to demonstration, he does not do so in his treatment of dialectic or rhetoric.

Ethics, and the common Axioms assumed in all the sciences, as discriminated from what is special and peculiar to each.[75]

Even the common belief that the contents of rhetoric and dialectic are limited to the contingent and probable is an exaggeration; for in each place that Aristotle discusses the point he includes a qualifier such as "usually." Of the two arts, the broader is dialectic, which Cope calls "the mother science of probable reasoning which handles every question."[76] "Rhetoric," he says, ". . .argues practical questions of politics and Ethics."[77]

Third, although Aristotle did not deny to the nonscientific reasoner the use of certainties when they would be helpful, he clearly regarded opinions and probabilities as the usual substance of dialectical and rhetorical discourse. In the *Rhetoric*, as a later section on the enthymeme indicates, he states repeatedly that the substance of premises is usually opinions or probabilities, and in the opening chapter of the *Topics* he clearly contrasts demonstration and dialectic:

> (*a*) It is a "demonstration", when the premises from which the reasoning starts are true and primary, or are such that our knowledge of them has originally come through premises which are primary and true; (*b*) reasoning, on the other hand, is "dialectical", if it reasons from opinions that are generally accepted. . . . those opinions are "generally accepted" which are accepted by every one or by the majority or by the philosophers.[78]

The expansion of this characterization of dialectical reasoning emphasizes the view that the subject matter appropriate to dialectic must be debatable. "For it is not every proposition nor yet every problem that is to be set down as dialectical: for no one in his senses would make a proposition of what no one holds, nor yet make a problem of what is obvious to everybody or to most people: for the latter admits of no doubt, while to the former no one would assent."[79] Shortly thereafter, perhaps consciously ap-

75. P. 393.
76. P. 91.
77. P. 91.
78. 100^{a}27-^{b}23. The following description of two other types of reasoning is not relevant to the present purpose. See also *Post. An.* i.33.88^b 30 -89^{a}1.
79. *Top.* i.10.104^{a}4 -8. See also i.11.104^{b}3 -16.

plying the doctrine of the mean, Aristotle locates the subject matter of dialectic in a very broad area between the two extremes already implied: "The subjects should not border too closely upon the sphere of demonstration, nor yet be too far removed from it: for the former cases admit of no doubt, while the latter involve difficulties too great."[80]

Fourth, the premises of rhetoric and dialectic differ from those of demonstration in the method by which they are secured. Whereas in scientific deduction the reasoner considers only the requirements of the proposition as he searches for truth or devises a proof for it, in rhetoric and dialectic interactions with other human beings largely determine premises. Although the orator and the dialectician influence thought through arguments and questions respectively, the effective premises in oratory are those that the listener creates in his mind[81] and the premises in dialectic are those that the respondent verbalizes. In the latter art the form and the conventions make the listener at least a partner in the creation of premises. No matter how canny the questioner, he must utilize whichever answer the respondent gives.

In conclusion, whereas the demonstrative premise must conform to rigid requirements and is chosen by the reasoner, the nondemonstrative premise has few limitations as to substance and is created jointly as reasoner and respondent or audience interact. The demonstrative premise must be a certainty, but the nondemonstrative may be whatever serves expediency. In both demonstration and nonscientific discourse the reasoner may form new premises by manipulating old ones, but the limitations for the two kinds of deduction are not the same. In science the limitation is what formal rules permit; in rhetoric, what the listener will accept; in dialectic, what the procedural rules approve.[82]

So the differences between the subject matter of demonstration and that of nonscience are important, but the distinctions in purpose go even deeper. Aristotle closes his basic treatment of the

80. i.11.105^{a}7 -9.

81. See the following section of this chapter on "The Enthymeme."

82. See esp. *Top.* viii.11. The use of right method may be more important than the use of true premises. See also *Top.* viii.12.162^{b}22 -30. Moreover, the nature of approved practices depends upon which of the three purposes of dialectic the dialogue aims to fulfill. See *Top.* i.2 and viii.5.159^{a}25 -38.

substance of dialectic by observing that the same topic may be treated either philosophically according to truth or dialectically according to general opinion.[83] The systems of demonstration, dialectic, and rhetoric, taken together, provide the individual with the means of dealing with all of the important types of material for three sets of purposes, which combined constituted the major intellectual activities of the Greek citizen. To teach the citizen when each of the three systems would be appropriate was an important task, and in this endeavor Aristotle was reasonably clear. A fourth system of thought and communication, imaginative or poetic discourse, differed so radically in material that confusion between it and any of the other three was unlikely.

THE ENTHYMEME

"Enthymemes," Aristotle states in his criticism of his predecessors, "are the substance of rhetorical persuasion."[84] "Every one who effects persuasion through proof does in fact use either enthymemes or examples: there is no other way."[85] So fundamental is the enthymeme to Aristotle's rhetoric, so elusive is the precise character of this adaptation of deduction, and so controversial has the nature of the enthymeme become, that a special section is appropriate. The purposes of the following pages are to consider the materials of the enthymeme, to assess the conflicting theories, and to draw conclusions that characterize this deductive form. Obviously "The enthymeme is a sort of syllogism,"[86] and Aristotle makes it clear in a number of places that it is the counterpart of scientific demonstration and the dialectical syllogism. But beyond this point the enthymeme becomes blurred. "The enthymeme is discussed in many passages in the *Rhetoric*,

83. *Ibid.*, i.14.105^{b}30 -31.
84. *Rhetoric* i.1.1354^{a}14 -15. The translation is by W. Rhys Roberts.
85. *Ibid.*, i.2.1356^{b}5 -7
86. *Ibid.*, i.1.1355^{a}5. Aristotle expands upon this statement in a passage in i.2 that stands as his clearest and most detailed formal definition: "...when it is shown that, certain propositions being true, a further and quite distinct proposition must also be true in consequence, whether invariably or usually, this is called syllogism in dialectic, enthymeme in rhetoric." 1356^{b}14 -17.

and it is impossible to extract from them a completely consistent theory of its nature."[87] Modern writers have increased the confusion.

Kinds of Material

Two statements can be made about the kinds of material. The first is that both general and specific materials are usable. "Enthymemes are of two main kinds," says W. David Ross. "There are the specific arguments dealing with the subject-matter of some science, e.g. ethics or physics, and the general arguments drawn from the *topoi.* "[88] Book i, chapters 4 -15, of the *Rhetoric* provide instruction on ideas and sources of ideas for enthymemes for each of the three types of oratory, and Book ii, chapters 19 and 23, are on the common *topoi.* A parallel exists between these two broad kinds of material for the enthymeme and the subject matter for demonstration, which consists of axioms suitable to the sciences generally and of premises specific to the science under consideration.

Differences in material, however, are not hard to find. The first, already mentioned, is that premises in demonstration must come from a particular genus whereas in rhetorical discourse there is no comparable limitation. The test is not any formal requirement but whether ideas as perceived by listeners are combined logically.

The second major difference in content is that the enthymeme may be based on probabilities, but a misconception here is prevalent. Although it is true that the enthymeme characteristically deals with probabilities, the orator is to use certainties when they are the materials that best fit his persuasive needs. Aristotle expresses this idea so often and so plainly that popularity of the notion that enthymemes *must* deal in probabilities is hard to understand. The "enthymeme and the examples must, then, deal with what is *in the main* contingent."[89] "There are *few* facts of the 'necessary' type that can form the basis of rhetorical syl-

87. W. D. Ross, *Aristotle's Prior and Posterior Analytics* (Oxford: Clarendon Press, 1965), p.409.

88. *Aristotle* (London: Methuen & Co., 1949), p.271.

89. *Rhet.* i.2.1357[a]14 -15. Italics by the writer.

logisms."[90] "We should also base our arguments upon probabilities as well as upon certainties."[91] ". . .the propositions forming the basis of enthymemes, though some of them may be 'necessary', will most of them be only usually true."[92]

So many clear and consistent statements leave no doubt about Aristotle's true position. Any other stand, moreover, would be incompatible with the broad pragmatism of the *Rhetoric*. As so often stated, the purpose was to tell students what would work for them as they sought "the available means of persuasion." Limiting the resources by drawing an arbitrary line between the subject matter of demonstration and that of rhetoric would have been un-Aristotelian. Why, then, has there been so much confusion? [93] The main reason, the writer suspects, is that the failure of competent scholars to verbalize the distinction between *usually* and *always* has misled readers, who have accepted careless statements without going to the *Rhetoric* themselves. A second possibility is that the heavy concentration of the *Rhetoric* on probable materials has been misleading. The only passages dealing with certain premises seem to be two in ii.25 (see 1402^b18 -19 and 1403^a10 -16) and one in i.2 (see 1357^b1 -17). A third possible explanation for the confusion is Aristotle's statement in both the *Prior Analytics*[94] and the *Rhetoric*[95] that enthymemes are based

90. *Ibid.*, i.2.1357^a22 -23. Italics by the writer.

91. *Ibid.*, ii.22.1396^a3 -4. Richard C. Jebb translates in these words: "And we must reason, not exclusively from necessary premises, but also from merely probable premises." In John Edwin Sandys, ed., *The Rhetoric of Aristotle* (Cambridge: At the University Press, 1909).

92. *Ibid.*, i.2.1357^a30 -32.

93. Edmund Cope makes probability the distinguishing characteristic of the enthymeme in numerous places, including pp. 102, 103, 154, and 221, and similar statements appear in recent publications. See Ray Nadeau, "Some Aristotelian and Stoic Influences on the Theory of Stases," *Speech Monographs,* XXVI (Nov., 1959), 252; and Charles S. Mudd, "The Enthymeme and Logical Vallidity," *Quarterly Journal of Speech,* XLV (Dec., 1959), 414. Cope, however, on p. 159 presents the view with which this writer agrees: "The materials or propositions of which enthythemes are constructed are only in very rare cases 'necessary.' "

94. ii.27.70^a3 -12.

95. i.2.1357^a32 -$^b21$. Both this passage and the one in the *Analytics* define *probability* and *sign* and discuss their uses.

upon probabilities and signs. The hasty reader can easily overlook the elaboration in the *Rhetoric*, which distinguishes between fallible and infallible signs and explains the latter as certainties. He also can fail to note the treatment in ii.25, which lists infallible signs as one of the four sources of enthymemes and again defines them as necessary:

> Enthymemes are derived from four sources; these are: (1) Probabilities, (2) Examples, (3) Infallible Signs, (4) Ordinary Signs. (1) Enthymemes taken from Probabilities are those which argue from what as a rule is or is thought to be true. (2) Enthymemes taken from Examples are those which proceed by induction from one or more parallel cases until the speaker abstracts a general rule, from which he then argues to the case in point. (3) Enthymemes taken from Infallible Signs are those which proceed from what is necessarily and invariably true. (4) Enthymemes taken from Fallible Signs are those which proceed from what is generally or partly true — possibly so, possibly not.[96]

In conclusion, the common belief that the enthymeme deals only with generalities and probabilities is an error. Rather, its materials at times, though neither often nor characteristically, are specific facts, infallible signs, and other sources of necessary premises. The subjects with which orators deal usually render a probability a more common premise than a certainty, but the good rhetorician uses whatever is best in the given circumstance.[97]

96. 1402[b]13 -21. The translation by J. E. C. Welldon gives the four materials of enthymemes as probabilities, examples, demonstrations, and signs. The translations of Jebb and Roberts, however, agree on this point with Cooper's, which is the one cited. Welldon's divergence is more than the substitution of one term for another, for the passage reads in part "[materials of the enthymeme are] demonstration when it depends upon a rule which is necessary and absolute; signs, when upon general or particular statements which may be either true or false."

97. One additional source that Aristotle specifically relates to the enthymeme is the maxim. The key passage is the following: "It [a maxim] is a statement . . .of a general kind; nor is it about any and every subject . . . but only about questions of practical conduct, courses of conduct to be chosen or avoided. Now an Enthymeme is a syllogism dealing with such practical subjects. It is therefore roughly true that the premises or conclusions of Enthymemes, considered apart from the rest of the argument, are Maxims. . . . Here we have a Maxim; add the reason or explanation and the whole thing is an Enthymeme." *Rhetoric* ii.20.1394[a]22 -32.

Conflicting Theories

Despite Aristotle's clarity and consistency on many features of the enthymeme, controversy about its nature has been extensive. Misunderstanding is the source of much of the disagreement, but misguided efforts to identify *a* particular quality as characterizing the enthymeme have been a special reason for confusion. The following paragraphs are an examination of the most prominent theories about the nature of the enthymeme.

First, a common assertion is that the enthymeme deals in probabilities whereas scientific demonstration starts with necessary premises and ends with necessary conclusions. As the preceding pages point out, this distinction holds in most instances but not universally.

Second, the enthymeme frequently is defined as an elided syllogism. Many contemporary speech textbooks, including some by well-known authors, make this statement, and the greatly respected Cope, although he qualifies his position in some passages, seems to regard elision as the fundamental characteristic:

> Plainly the difference between the two latter [dialectical syllogism and rhetorical enthymemes] is one of *form*. The syllogism is complete in all its parts; the enthymeme incomplete; one of the premisses or the conclusion is *invariably* wanting. If further proof were needed, it would be found in this, that the relation of the example to induction is precisely similar.[98]

Those who define the enthymeme as an elided syllogism, thus, belong to a distinguished company. The error, as with probability, lies in mistaking a quality that commonly is true for one that is universal. The mistake, according to R. C. Jebb, originated long ago,[99] and so far all attempts to correct the miscon-

98. P. 103. The italics are by Cope. Also: "The enthymeme differs from the strict dialectical syllogism only in *form*. . . . The difference between the two is simply this, that the dialectician rigorously maintains the form of the syllogism, with its three propositions, major and minor premiss and conclusion: the rhetorician *never* expresses all three — if he did, his enthymeme would become a regular syllogism." P. 221.

99. "A misapprehension of Aristotle's meaning had, as early as the first century B. C., led to the conception of the enthymeme as not merely a syllogism of a particular subject matter, but also a syllogism of which one premise is suppressed." *Attic Orators,* Vol. II (London, 1876), p. 291.

ception have been ineffective. The emphasis on formal deficiency in Aristotle's explanations and the presence of truncated examples of the enthymeme no doubt contribute to the perpetuation of the false belief.

From the truth that enthymemes usually are incomplete in expression to the conclusion that elision is their fundamental feature is an unwarranted leap for two reasons: (1) No evidence exists to support the position that Aristotle defines the enthymeme as an elided syllogism. The writer finds none in the *Rhetoric*, and neither did James H. McBurney, who made a special study of the enthymeme:

> There appears to be no place in Aristotle's writings where he defines the enthymeme as an elided syllogism, nor is there any satisfactory evidence that he so understood it. In his discussion of *maxims* and in many other places, Aristotle recognizes the enthymeme with one or more of its propositions suppressed; as a matter of fact, I think we can safely interpret Aristotle to mean that the enthymeme *usually* lacks one or more of the propositions of a complete syllogism. On the other hand, it seems equally clear that there is no justification in interpreting him to mean that this is a necessary characteristic of the enthymeme.[100]

(2) Expediency, not logic, explains the presence of elision as a feature. The instruction on creating and presenting enthymemes, like the rest of the *Rhetoric*, is in a practical context. "The enthymeme must consist of few propositions, fewer often than those which make up the normal syllogism. For if any of these propositions is a familiar fact, there is no need even to mention it; the hearer adds it himself."[101] The number of propositions or premises, it should be noted, is not *always* fewer but *often* fewer, and whether a premise is to be stated or omitted depends not on any formal characteristic of the enthymeme but on whether the audience is likely to supply what is missing. In Book ii Aristotle adds to this line of thought when he states that the purpose of elision is to avoid confusion and save words: ". . .we must not carry its [the enthymeme's] reasoning too far back, or the length of our argument will cause obscurity: nor must we put in all the

100. "The Place of the Enthymeme in Rhetorical Theory," *Speech Monographs*, III (1936), 67.
101. i.2.1357^{a}16-19.

steps that lead to our conclusion, or we shall waste words in saying what is manifest."[102] Likewise in Book iii, the reason for elision is practical — audience adaptation — and not formal: "You cannot ask a series of questions owing to the incapacity of the audience to follow them; and for this reason you should also make your enthymemes as compact as possible."[103]

Third, some scholars hold that the distinctive characteristic of the enthymeme is that the audience supplies one premise. An article by Lloyd F. Bitzer in 1959 has been the most persuasive presentation of this view,[104] but the idea appears in writings as far back as Minucian[105] and as recent as Cope,[106] McBurney,[107] and Charles S. Mudd.[108]

The evidence for this view, of course, had been in the *Rhetoric* all along. ". . .we must use, as our modes of persuasion and argument, notions possessed by everybody, as we observed in the *Topics* when dealing with the way to handle a popular audience."[109] "We must not, therefore, start from any and every accepted opinion, but only from those we have defined — those accepted by our judges or by those whose authority they recog-

102. ii.22.1395[b]24 -28.

103. iii.18.1419[a]17 -19.

104. "Aristotle's Enthymeme Revisited," *Quarterly Journal of Speech*, XLV (Dec., 1959), 399 -408.

105. "The enthymemes are so-called either because the orator himself invented them and develops them in the mind (*enthymo*), or because he depends on the jurors to consider the matter further in their minds if he omits something. The rhetorical syllogisms have omissions; they differ from the syllogisms in philosophy in that the latter lead directly to conclusions while the former leave the conclusions drawn from the premises and postulations to be considered further by the juror." Prentice A. Meador, Jr., "Minucian, On Epicheiremes: An Introduction and a Translation," *Speech Monographs*, XXXI (March, 1964), 59. This passage comes from the Greek text in Leonard Spengel, ed., *Rhetores Graeci* (Leipzig: Teubner, 1853), I, 419.

106. Pp. 93 -158.

107. P. 63.

108. P. 414. This article is in the same issue as the one by Bitzer.

109. i.1.1355[a]27 -29. The passage in the *Topics* is i.2.101[a]30 -34.

nize."[110] ". . .the materials of syllogisms are the ordinary opinions of men."[111]

Bitzer, who includes the three preceding citations in his article, closes as follows:

> This view holds that the enthymeme succeeds as an instrument of rational persuasion because its premises are always drawn from the audience. Accordingly, I offer the following as a tentative and exploratory definition. The enthymeme is a syllogism based on probabilities, signs, and examples, whose function is rhetorical persuasion. Its successful construction is accomplished through the joint efforts of speaker and audience, and this is its essential character.[112]

The phrase "always drawn from the audience" is questionable, as the word *usually* should be placed between "syllogism" and "based."

Fourth, Lane Cooper appears to regard an enthymeme as any persuasive argument regardless of length or formal complexity. This position, which the following quotation presents, is vague, but the essential point is more nearly consistent with the heart of Aristotle's concept of rhetoric than are the characterizations that stress probability, elision, or audience participation. Whereas these three approaches look to the outward qualities of the enthymeme for clues concerning its essence, Cooper's definition reaches for the fundamental characteristics of the *Rhetoric* itself:

> Enthymemes are the essential instrument of oratorical persuasion. He [Aristotle] says, too, that they are a kind of syllogism. Yet many students of the *Rhetoric,* including learned men, and some professed logicians, do not seem to realize where Aristotle found his syllogisms or his enthymemes, or where, accordingly, we should look for them. Somewhere, of course, if they really exist as living forms, they must have each of them its natural habitat. . . . In the *Rhetoric,* again, the analysis of enthymemes is quite properly anatomical . . . . an enthymeme may be a maxim of one term; so Lincoln's "All men are created equal." Or, again, it may be a maxim of two terms, yet not syllogistic; such are all the Beatitudes: 'Blessed are the pure in heart, for they shall see God.' The arguments good speakers actually use in persuasion are enthymemes.

110. *Rhetoric* ii.22.1395^{b}32 -1396^{a}1.
111. *Ibid.,* ii.25.1402^{a}32 -33.
112. P. 408.

That, then, is the answer to our question, "What is an enthymeme?" It is a thing one can find in a place; it is the kind of argument used by St. Paul or by Lincoln in a speech. The place in which to look for good enthymemes is a good speech, as the place in which to look for syllogisms is a tight scientific argument. . . . In a narrow sense, an enthymeme is one link in a persuasive argument; more loosely, and commonly, it is a short chain. . . .

Aristotle, writing compactly, gives examples when he thinks them needed, but does not give a complete example of the enthymematic process, though of course he refers to many single enthymemes.[113]

Conclusions

The following are the writer's conclusions:

1. The characterization of the enthymeme should be multidimensional. Attempts to define it by reference to a single characteristic are oversimplifications, and the search for a single quality that alone differentiates the enthymeme from other deductive forms leads scholars beyond tenable positions. No need exists for finding *the* characteristic, and the only value of these inquiries has been a stimulation of interest.

2. The purpose of the enthymeme is to persuade, and the context of the *Rhetoric* is practical. Aristotle probably intended to give the enthymeme the broadest possible definition consistent with its practical persuasive function.

3. One dimension of the enthymeme is the material upon which it is based. Since those who apply rhetoric deal typically with policies in the realm of human affairs, the materials usually are probabilities rather than certainties. No evidence exists, however, to indicate that Aristotle ruled out the use of necessary premises.

4. A second dimension of the enthymeme is its form. Usually it is elided, but there is no proof that it must be. The reasons for truncation are practical and not formal — clarity rarely requires the verbalization of all three propositions, and a simple, brief expression usually seems less pedantic and is more effective than a complex, lengthy presentation.

113. "Introduction" in *The Rhetoric of Aristotle* (New York: Appleton-Century-Crofts, 1932), pp. xxv-xxvii.

5. A third dimension is the source of premises. Frequently the audience provides one premise, but no evidence exists to show that premises must always coincide with preexisting beliefs. Utilizing the attitudes of listeners is sound persuasion, but Aristotle does not make this procedure a universal.

6. The enthymeme uses whatever materials are the most suitable to the circumstances. Among these materials are probabilities, examples, infallible signs, and fallible signs.

7. The enthymeme is a deductive form whose purpose in rhetoric is comparable to the objectives of demonstration in science and of the dialectical syllogism in dialectic. Each of the three forms of the syllogism is an instrument for achieving the purposes peculiar to its own particular field. Thus, demonstration arrives at a necessary conclusion, whereas the dialectical syllogism is an instrument for seeking probable truth. The objective of the enthymeme is persuasion.

Thus, in the final analysis the distinctive characteristics of the enthymeme are derived from the art to which it pertains — rhetoric — and from the aim which it is to serve — persuasion. The best one-sentence definition is this: An enthymeme is any deductive argument employed to further the communicator's persuasive ends.[114] This definition may seem at first to be too simple to be useful, but its focus is right — on the end that deduction serves in rhetorical discourse. Moreover, being general, it includes all aspects of the Aristotelian doctrine.

SIGNS

Finally, to complete this analysis of the substance of Aristotle's deduction one must examine his treatment of signs. In earlier parts of the chapter fallible and infallible signs have been listed as materials for the enthymeme, and the latter type, because it deals in certainty, also is suitable for demonstration. The placing of the most detailed treatment in the *Prior Analytics*, a more general logical work than the *Posterior Analytics,* indicates that

114. This definition is similar to one published by Gary L. Cronkhite while the present work was in preparation. See "The Enthymeme as Deductive Rhetorical Argument," *Western Speech*, XXX (Spring, 1966), 133.

signs are materials for both demonstrative and nonscientific thought. In ii.27 Aristotle defines the fallible and the infallible types[115] and takes up problems of both form and substance. He fails to focus, however, upon the critical point, which is whether outward appearance bears an invariable relation to inner quality. The following passage is as definite as any, but even in it the contingencies are so numerous that the guidance to the receiver is slight:

> It is possible to infer character from features, if it is granted that the body and the soul are changed together by the natural affections: . . . I refer to passions and desires when I speak of natural motions. If then this were granted and also that for each change there is a corresponding sign, and we could state the affection and sign proper to each kind of animal, we shall be able to infer character from features.[116]

How one knows whether a sign is infallible is unsolved in the *Prior Analytics,* and the possibility that fallible signs may have differing degrees of probability is not considered.

The other treatments of sign also leave these basic problems unsettled, but are informative in other ways. Only infallible signs, as several passages state[117] and as the nature of demonstration obviously requires, are satisfactory in scientific thought, and even they are inferior to causes as starting points for reasoning. This inferiority of knowing the sign to knowing the cause is the principal point made about signs in the *Posterior Analytics.* Proof through signs, according to this work, ". . . though the conclusion be actually essential, one will not know it as essential nor know its reason; but to have reasoned knowledge of a conclusion is to know it through its cause."[118] In Aristotle's system, let it be remembered, knowing the cause was a requirement for real knowledge.[119]

The *Rhetoric* in passages in i.2, i.3, ii.24, and ii.25, as would be expected, examines signs as a means of persuasion. The deve-

---

115. His famous examples are these: argument from infallible sign, ". . .that a woman is with child because she has milk"; argument from fallible sign, "The proof that a woman is with child because she is pale." 70^a13 -21.
116. 70^b6 -13.
117. *Rhetoric* i.2.1357^b3 -6, 14 -17; ii.25.1403^a3 -4, 10 -16.
118. i.6.75^a33 -36.
119. For example, see *Meta.* i.1.981^a23 -$^b5$.

lopment contains no surprises to one familiar with the *Analytics*. Infallible signs cannot be refuted, but those that are fallible are refutable;[120] sign even is listed as the fourth sham enthymeme.[121] Beyond these points, there are only matters already mentioned — definitions of fallible and infallible signs, the connection of the latter with complete proof, and the inclusion of signs in the analyses of the materials of enthymemes.

The major weaknesses of the entire presentation are (1) the false dichotomizing of a form of proof which is viewed more accurately as a continuum extending from coincidental relationship to certainty and (2) the failure to develop any useful procedures and tests for determining infallibility. Some contributions, on the other hand, are important. (1) That man reasons on the basis of the outward manifestations that he perceives was an astute observation, and without the inclusion of sign the treatment of deduction as a real-life activity would be incomplete. (2) The classification of signs into fallible and infallible directed attention, though not pointedly enough, toward the problem of the relation of external manifestation to inner reality.

The weaknesses in Aristotle's treatment may lie in the inherent difficulties of the topic. Scholars in the more than two thousand years since his time have left the critical problems unsolved, and most discussions have been less complete, clear, and provocative than his.

CONCLUSION

Man's most distinctive accomplishment is reasoning, and the most highly developed method of thought is deduction. To this day the supreme analyst of this form is Aristotle. This chapter has been an examination of his writings for answers to a broad question crucial to any analysis of his deductive system, "What does man reason about? "

The answers to this question for demonstration differ from those for dialectic and rhetoric, both nonsciences. Consistency marks Aristotle's writings here as it does throughout his system.

120. *Rhetoric* ii.25.1403^{a}3 -4, 10 -16.
121. *Ibid.,* ii.24.1401^{b}9 -13. Here as elsewhere whenever Aristotle uses "sign" without a modifier he means the fallible type.

For each of the three types of deduction subject matter, purpose, and distinctive nature interrelate with the type of material that is acceptable for the premises. That demonstration proceeds only from certain, necessary, invariable materials is the obvious example, but the congruity between purpose and subject matter is true also for dialectic and rhetoric.

In probing the nature of materials and premises, one comes close to the essence of the deductive process. The primary questions that demonstration tests are "Is ———— a fact? " and "Does ———— exist? " The two secondary questions are of cause and essence. To answer these questions the reasoner constructs syllogisms made of two kinds of material: (1) axioms applicable to the sciences generally; and (2) premises drawn from the science within whose genus the inquiry lies. In the pursuance of the deductive process terms must be defined properly, and premises must be constructed that are true, necessary, essential, commensurately universal, primary, prior in nature, and causal. A secondary purpose of the chapter is to explain these qualities, which are critical to understanding Aristotle's deduction.

The second half of the chapter pertains to non-scientific deduction and especially to the enthymeme. This deductive instrument, according to Aristotle, is the principal and indispensable instrument of rhetorical discourse. An accurate understanding of the enthymeme, therefore, is necessary if one is to grasp the nature of rhetoric. Since the most widely held theories are inaccurate, a summarzing list of seven points is an important corrective.

Deduction, of course, is only one of the two types of reasoning. The following chapter brings together into a system Aristotle's scattered and fragmentary remarks on induction.

CHAPTER 4

Induction

Aristotle's treatment of induction must be included in any thorough exposition of his logic. Although the common belief that his induction is incomplete, unsystematic, and generally unsatisfactory as compared with his deduction is well justified, induction still is vital to the total system of scientific thought and is important in many ways to rhetoric and dialectic. Moreover, without induction the scientific system, as explained in the preceding chapter, would have no starting place.

To point out that the first principles upon which demonstration rests come through inductive processes is to say less than enough, for the intertwining of induction and deduction is more basic than the statement suggests. They form a whole; together they are science; in real situations neither can function alone. Observations followed by induction lead to hypotheses, the scientific thinker uses dialectic method to examine these hypotheses for acceptability as first principles, and only then can he begin the deductive stages with their attention to causes and formal rules. And throughout there is a continual application of common sense and a checking of the reasoned results with actuality.[1] So the total system, although the striking elaboration of syllogistic rules may suggest otherwise, is a closely knit entity in which observation,

---

1. "The effort in any scientific analysis is to proceed from the facts of sense experience to those things better known in nature which may serve as principles for general scientific proof. The possibility of scientific demonstration depends on knowledge of first principles.... In any case of conflict between theory and empirical data, formal preconceptions must be abandoned in favor of adherence to facts. Not only are the principles of all sciences derived originally by induction from experience, but they are checked ultimately by their adequacy to account for phenomena." Richard McKeon, "Aristotle's Conception of the Development and the Nature of Scientific Method," *Journal of the History of Ideas*, VIII (Jan., 1947), 39.

induction, dialectical thought, formal deduction and causal reasoning, common sense, and further observation are all indispensable.

Induction, therefore, is well worth studying, but the problems for the analyst are formidable. Nowhere does Aristotle present a coherent, detailed account or even a pattern that the scholar can adopt as a guide for pulling together the scattered ideas. The traditional response has been to say that Aristotle's induction is disorganized and incomplete, but this generalization may be a half-truth that has discouraged attempts to arrive at constructive judgments. Perhaps a study of the scattered passages may yield a more highly developed and more systematic body of theory than has been generally acknowledged. The only possible method to follow is to examine numerous widely separated passages, analyze these materials and collate the ideas, engage in a certain amount of inference drawing, and finally, if all goes well, synthesize. The kinds of resources for this effort are twofold. First, numerous statements specify in bits and pieces Aristotle's ideas on the nature, the values, and the uses of the several inductive forms. Second, the illustrations of these points sometimes tell the careful analyst more than does the exposition. The pages that follow are an attempt to contribute to the literature on Aristotle's induction by a utilization of both kinds of resource.

.Perhaps such a construction from the separated items will be a distortion -- an attribution of system and implications of significance that Aristotle neither provides nor intended. Although this point is important and is critical to maintaining the proper perspective, the values of a systematized view of induction seem to outweigh any objections. Indeed, synthesizing the scattered remarks may be the only way to correct the widely held viewpoint that the following passage by George Grote typifies:

> Upon this foundation he erects the superstructure of Science; the universal propositions acquired through Induction, and applied again to particulars or to lower generalities, through the rules of the deductive Syllogism. He signalizes, with just emphasis, the universalizing point of view called Science or Theory; but he regards it as emerging from particular facts, and as travelling again downwards toward particular facts. The misfortune is, that he contents himself with barely recognizing, though he distinctly proclaims the necessity of, the inductive part of this complex operation. . . . one half of Logic is made to

look like the whole; Science is disjoined from Experience, and is presented as consisting in Deduction alone.[2]

ARISTOTLE AS A MAN OF SCIENCE

One other important introductory point is Aristotle's training in science and his use of its methods in many of his scholarly activities. In his boyhead at the court of Philip of Macedon, as various biographers report, he learned the research methods of the physicians, and an inspection of his extant scientific works indicates that observation and classification were lifelong activities. "More of a man of science than Plato, Aristotle conceived the idea of constructing an encyclopedia of all knowledge; and with the aid of his College of research students he carried the plan to completion. This gives him his position as the father of European science . . . . Darwin wrote, 'Linnaeus and Cuvier have been my two gods . . . but they were children to old Aristotle.' "[3]

For a man so predisposed to observation and research, the likelihood was particularly great that induction would have a major role in his overall scientific system and in his development of rhetoric and dialectic. A predisposition toward investigation, however, does not guarantee that a theory of induction will be satisfactory, and the frequent practice of scientific research does not make a methodology of high order inevitable. Moreover, the statement that Aristotle knew and practiced inductive method does not mean that these were his only intellectual processes. To the contrary, much of his work on communication was the product of theorizing without any obvious observational foundation. Induction is significant to the whole, but the importance should not be overemphasized.

GENERAL THEORY

How can Aristotle's induction be characterized? The first

2. *Aristotle*, ed. Alexander Bain and G. C. Robertson (London, 1883), p.199.
3. Harris Rackham, "Introduction," in *Aristotle's Ethics for English Readers* (Oxford: Basil Blackwell, 1944), p. 7.

step toward the construction of a coherent exposition is to present the general treatment given to this part of his logic. As a beginning, Aristotle discusses several kinds of induction and these collectively broaden considerably the basic definition expressed in the tidy contrast "Thus demonstration develops from universals, induction from particulars."[4]

First and most familiarly, *induction* is the process of attaining certainty through complete enumeration. "For induction proceeds," Aristotle states, "through an enumeration of all the cases."[5] This declaration is consistent with the scientific ideal but not with the less rigorous requirements for rhetoric and dialectic. In fact, Aristotle's own applications of the inductive process often show a relaxed standard. Thus, in the *Topics* i.12 he illustrates induction by citing two instances and drawing a generalization,[6] and in the *Rhetoric* ii.23 he illustrates the *topos* induction with a succession of examples in which conclusions rest upon three, two, six, and three instances respectively.[7] No disclaimer is added to suggest that these are not satisfactory models, and the combining of strengthening devices with each of these lists of instances suggests that Aristotle may have recognized that the inductive support alone was inadequate. This conclusion seems particularly true for rhetoric. An analysis of his examples shows that he judged the adequacy of induction by the totality of the argument and that the extent to which the enumeration was complete was only one of several unstated criteria.

Different standards for nonscientific and scientific induction are not surprising, and in many instances the looser procedures with their multicriteria and their "leaps" from data to conclusion are the more useful. A complete induction in which the generalization is coextensive with the sum of its instances, nevertheless, also is of value. The verbalization of a general truth shows that the reasoner has perceived a rational relation in his data, whereas a series of individual statements is at most raw material

4. *Posterior Analytics* i.18.81[a]40 -[b]1. The translation is by G. R. G. Mure. See also the *Topics* i.12.105[a]13. The translation is by W. A. Pickard-Cambridge.

5. *Prior Analytics* ii.23.68[b]28-29. The translation is by A. J. Jenkinson.

6. The two instances are species, not individuals. 105[a]13 -16.

7. 1398[a]32 -[b]18. The translation is by W. Rhys Roberts.

for analysis. The general statement, also, is usable as a premise, whereas an assembly of individual instances is not.

Second, induction is a process of generalizing on the basis of qualities common to species. Whereas some of Aristotle's examples deal with individuals, a greater number pertain to species. Such is the case in the *Prior Analytics* ii.23, in the *Topics* i.12, and in three of the four illustrations in the *Rhetoric* ii.23. This modification of induction based on particulars adds greatly to the flexibility of this form of reasoning and must have helped to bring the description into accord with everyday Greek practice. Working with species rather than individual instances, however, creates an added hazard, for the inductive process leading to the generalization about each of the species could be faulty. Nowhere in the material labeled as dealing with induction does Aristotle consider this problem or note that proceeding from species is in effect an induction based on a lower order induction. It is a passage on definition that describes this double inductive process accurately and that is at least suggestive of a methodology:

> To resume our account of the right method of investigation: We must start by observing a set of similar — i.e. specifically identical — individuals, and consider what element they have in common. We must then apply the same process to another set of individuals which belong to one species and are generically but not specifically identical with the former set. When we have established what the common element is in all members of this second species, and likewise in members of further species, we should again consider whether the results established possess any identity, and persevere until we reach a single formula, since this will be the definition of the thing.[8]

Noteworthy concerning the treatment in the *Rhetoric* of these two forms of induction — generalizations based on individual instances and on species respectively — is the combining of inductive arguments with other devices to form probative units. Of the four illustrations cited in the passage on the *topos* induction, three employ such supporting devices. The second includes the claim that all other instances support the conclusion, the third uses a series of *a fortiori* ideas, and the fourth expresses time relationships to add credibility to the implied cause-effect connection.

Third, the term *induction* in some places in Aristotle's

8. *Post. An.* ii.13.97^{b}6 -13.

writings refers to a largely unstructured process leading to insight. The number of instances in this usage is not important; the stress is on the individual instance that leads to perceiving the universal. This concept of induction, which is the one basic to an analysis of the process of apprehending the first premise, in Aristotle's system is the most important of all of the inductive uses.

> When one of a number of logically indiscriminable particulars has made a stand, the earliest universal is present in the soul: for though the act of sense-perception is of the particular, its content is universal . . . . A fresh stand is made among these rudimentary universals, and the process does not cease until the indivisible concepts, the true universals are established. . . .
>
> Thus it is clear that we must get to know the primary premisses by induction; for the method by which even sense-perception implants the universal is inductive.[9]

In all three of these inductive functions the movement is from known to unknown — a characteristic that Aristotle specifies and emphasizes. Not only do statements of this quality appear in a number of works,[10] but also the opening passage of the *Posterior Analytics*, Aristotle's major work on scientific method, stresses the movement from old knowledge to new in both syllogism and induction:

> All instruction given or received by way of argument proceeds from pre-existent knowledge. This becomes evident upon a survey of all the species of such instruction. The mathematical sciences and all other speculative disciplines are acquired in this way, and so are the two forms of dialectical reasoning, syllogistic and inductive; for each of these latter makes use of old knowledge to impart new, the syllogism assuming an audience that accepts its premisses, induction exhibiting the universal as implicit in the clearly known particular. Again, the persuasion exerted by rhetorical arguments is in principle the same.[11]

9. *Ibid.*, ii.19.100^{a}15 -^{b}5.

10. For example: "Induction should proceed from individual cases to the universal and from the known to the unknown; and the objects of perception are better known, to most people if not invariably." *Top.* viii.1.156^{a}4 -6. See also the *Metaphysics* i.9.992^{b}34. The translation is by W. D. Ross.

11. i.1.71^{a}1 -9.

Uses and Values of Induction

Several uses and values in addition to those implied in the preceding pages are worthy of mention. As compared with deduction, induction is clearer and more convincing, particularly when the respondent is the ordinary citizen. The reason for this appears in a passage asserting the superiority: "Induction is the more convincing and clear: it is more readily learnt by the use of the senses, and is applicable generally to the mass of men."[12] Elsewhere Aristotle states that "objects nearer to sense are prior and better known to man,"[13] and in the *Rhetoric* he speaks of the values of the example, especially the fable, over the enthymeme when listeners are not trained reasoners.[14]

In dialectical discourse, likewise, induction is of particular value in dealing with the crowd,[15] but in dialectic it also has true probative uses both extensive and varied. Aristotle advises the use of induction to secure arguments among contradictories,[16] to establish the topic of greater good,[17] to prove certain types of premise,[18] and to refute through contraries a use of genus.[19] Induction also is a method to employ in dealing with an opponent who refuses to grant a premise that the dialectician desires.[20]

Still other uses are mentioned for scientific thought. In situations in which no middle term exists and in which proof through the usual syllogism is impossible, induction is the proper tool.[21] Also in this chapter is a supposedly inductive syllogism in which the relation of one extreme to the middle is proved through

12. *Top.* i.12.105^{a}16 -18.

13. *Post. An.* i.2.72^{a}2. See also ii.23.68^{b}35 -37.

14. ii.20.1394^{a}2.

15. "In dialectics, syllogism should be employed in reasoning against dialecticians rather than against the crowd: induction, on the other hand, is most useful against the crowd." *Top.* viii.2.157^{a}19 -21. See also i.12. 105^{a}18 -19.

16. *Ibid.,* ii.8.113^{b}17.

17. *Ibid.,* ii.10.115^{a}3 -6.

18. *Ibid.,* iv.2.122^{a}17 -19.

19. *Ibid.,* iv.3.123^{b}7 -8.

20. *Ibid.,* viii.1.155^{b}33.

21. *Pr. An.* ii.23.68^{b}30 -32.

the other extreme.[22] This attempt to force induction into a syllogistic format accomplishes nothing and creates an involved, confusing explanation for an argument better explained as a generalization from a series of examples in which two qualities appear together.

Not at all forced 'are two other values that Aristotle assigns to induction. In the *Posterior Analytics* ii.5 he states that it is the means by which certain kinds of truth are made evident,[23] and two chapters later he specifies one "truth" of this type: ". . .induction proves not what the essential nature of a thing is but that it has or has not some attribute."[24] Although the language suggests that finding the essence is the higher and more worthy endeavor, a method that results in locating attributes also must be evaluated as important.

These, then, are values of induction when employed alone — clarity and persuasiveness, especially to the masses, an instrument to be preferred for its probative force in a variety of dialectical situations, a means of scientific proof when deduction is impossible, and a means of apprehending attributes.

Induction as an Adjunct of Deduction

The preceding list is impressive, but even so the role in Aristotle's system of induction by itself is relatively small. The amount of space in relation to the entire *Organon* is slight, the analyses do not appear in prominent positions, the treatment is not organized, and the case is not urged. One finds the uses and the values of induction only by a careful search.

The one function of induction that Aristotle clearly regards as important is that of serving as an adjunct to deduction. The dependence of the latter upon the former is clear and specific in Aristotle,[25] a point made elsewhere in this book and a feature that many scholars have observed. To labor the matter would be useless.

22. 68^b15 -29.
23. 91^b34 -35.
24. 92^a40 -$^b1$.
25. "Thus it is clear that we must get to know the primary premisses by induction; for the method by which even sense-perception implants the

Conclusion

A balanced view neither exaggerates the values that Aristotle gives to induction nor accepts fully the common belief that this form of reasoning lacks importance. Essential to demonstration, it also has some values of its own. For a full and accurate understanding of the uses of this logical form one must go beyond the passages labeled "induction." The following sections extend the present inquiry to Aristotle's treatment of example, analogy, and *a fortiori*.

EXAMPLE

A common belief is that the example is a rhetorical induction, and Aristotle's own statements[26] can be cited in support. This view, however, is not entirely accurate, for there are two passages in the *Organon*[27] that ascribe to the example properties and uses distinct from those of induction. One of these is a short passage in the *Prior Analytics* at ii.24.69^{a}13 -19, and the other is a lengthy statement that will be fully discussed in the next section. The important point at the moment is that to label "example" as "rhetorical induction" is neither very informative nor entirely true.

Characteristics of the Example

There is only one extended passage treating the example in the context of logic:

> We have an "example" when the major term is proved to belong to the middle by means of a term which resembles the third. It ought to be

universal is inductive." *Ibid.,* ii.19.100 ^{b}4 -5. Also: "Now induction is the starting-point which knowledge even of the universal presupposes, while syllogism proceeds *from* universals. There are therefore starting-points from which syllogism proceeds, which are not reached by syllogism; it is therefore by induction that they are acquired." *Nicomachean Ethics* vi.3.1139^{b}27 -30. The translation is by W. D. Ross.

26. *Post. An.* i.1.71^{a}8 -11; *Rhet.* i.2.1356^{b}4 -5, 13 -14.

27. The writer has seen no other, and Troy Organ, *An Index to Aristotle* (Princeton, N.J.: Princeton University Press, 1959), p. 56, lists no other.

known both that the middle belongs to the third term, and that the first belongs to that which resembles the third. . . . the belief in the relation of the middle term to the extreme should be produced by several similar cases. Clearly then to argue by example is neither like reasoning from part to whole, nor like reasoning from whole to part, but rather reasoning from part to part, when both particulars are subordinate to the same term, and one of them is known. It differs from induction, because induction starting from all the particular cases proves that the major term belongs to the middle, and does not apply the syllogistic conclusion to the minor term, whereas argument by example does make this application and does not draw its proof from all the particular cases.[28]

An analysis of the foregoing passage yields six characteristics: (1) that example is reasoning from one particular to another and thus is like the literal analogy in modern treatises; (2) that it moves from the known; (3) that the known particular and the inferred one belong to the same genus; (4) that it does not consider all cases; (5) that it proves that the major term belongs to the middle by means of a term that *resembles* the third term; and (6) that it applies the syllogistic conclusion to the minor term. All of these qualities except the second and the third differentiate the example from induction, and Aristotle, therefore, must have thought of the two terms as applying to separate forms of reasoning. This treatment creates an unanswered question. Aristotle states repeatedly that the only two forms of reasoning are induction and deduction, and he neither explains why example is not a third nor in what respects it is one of the other two. Much else, also, is unsaid; for instance, he does not state the circumstances under which example is useful, and he gives scant guidance for its employment. These omissions and the extremely small amount of space given the example in the *Organon* support the inference that to Aristotle the role of the example in the logical system for science is small.

Somewhat larger is the role in rhetoric. As in logic, example is a reasoning from part to part, from familiar to unfamiliar, and from one element to another within the same order; but in addition it is a reasoning from like to like,[29] and its overall

28. *Pr. An.* ii.24. 68^{b}38 -69^{a}19.
29. "The 'example' has already been described as one kind of induction:
. . .Its relation to the proposition it supports is not that of part to whole, nor

position is one of greater dignity than in logic. Instead of being something parallel to induction, it *is* rhetorical induction and as such is parallel to the enthymeme as one of the two possible logical methods:

> The example is an induction. . . . I call the enthymeme a rhetorical syllogism, and the example a rhetorical induction. . . . And since everyone who proves anything at all is bound to use either syllogisms or inductions (and this is clear to us from the *Analytics*), it must follow that enthymemes are syllogisms and examples are inductions. . . . When we base the proof of a proposition on a number of similar cases, this is induction in dialectic, example in rhetoric.[30]

The preceding passage clearly locates example within the total logical system for rhetoric, but what are its principal qualities?

First, a comparison of the passage apparently intended as definition in the *Rhetoric* (see footnote 29) and in the *Prior Analytics* (see the quotation on pp. 89-90) yields two differences in scope. The first of these, the specific exclusion of argument from whole to whole in the *Rhetoric,* probably has no significance and shows only that Aristotle did not always word his ideas the same way in one passage as in another. The overall nature of the scientific and the rhetorical systems makes it unlikely that this exclusion would be intended for the latter but not for the former.

whole to part, nor whole to whole, but of part to part, or like to like. When two statements are of the same order, but one is more familiar than the other, the former is an 'example'." *Rhet.* i.2.1357[b]25 -30. Cope's expansion is clearer than the foregoing translation by Roberts: "The example stands neither in the relation of part to whole (as in induction, by which the universal is gathered from the particular and individual), nor in that of whole to part (as in the opposite process of deduction or syllogism, which concludes from the universal to the particular), nor as whole to whole (the conclusion from universal to universal, likewise effected by syllogism), but in the relation of particular to particular, of like to like; when the example, and the analogous fact that is to be inferred from it, are both under (i.e. species of) the same genus, but the one is better known than the other." E. M. Cope, *Introduction to Aristotle's Rhetoric* (London, 1867), p. 165.

30. *Rhet.* i.2.1356[b]3 -14. A reference in the *Posterior Analytics* to rhetorical arguments identifies example as "a kind of induction" and as one of the two forms of argument. i.1.71[a]8 -10.

The addition of "like to like," on the other hand, probably is intentional, for it modifies the definition of the example of rhetoric in the expected direction — greater freedom. This addition is significant in that it adds the analogy of relations (mathematical analogy) to the analogy of things (logical analogy).

Second, the illustration of argument by example in the *Rhetoric* i.2 suggests that in practice this form of reasoning may be much like induction as that term is generally understood. To prove that "Dionysius in asking. . . for a bodyguard is scheming to make himself a despot," Aristotle names two instances in which such requests resulted in tyrrany. ". . .all other instances known to the speaker," he advises, "[should be] made into examples."[31] Although each instance taken separately is related to the point being proved as "part to part," the effect of the entire passage is to emphasize the persuasive value of many instances.

The treatment, nevertheless, is a shift from the position in logic that induction rests upon an examination of all instances. In rhetoric, so the illustrations indicate, the impossibility of a complete investigation does not rule out the use of example. Aristotle's practice, like that of modern speakers, is to offer several examples, to bolster the effect in whatever ways are suitable, and to follow no precise formula. Since the number of illustrations reflects no observable principle, how many he used in a given place may have depended on how many were in his memory.

Third, the example combines with the enthymeme in a fashion analogous to the relation in demonstration between induction and deduction. Aristotle's own description of the example-enthymeme unit, a part of the discussion of the "four kinds of alleged" facts upon which enthymemes may be based, is clear and concise: "Enthymemes based upon Examples are those which proceed by induction from one or more similar cases, arrive at a general proposition, and then argue deductively to a particular inference."[32]

Materials Used in Reasoning by Example

Further characterization of the example is possible through

31. 1357^b34.
32. *Rhet.* ii.25.1402^b16 -18.

an examination of the materials that Aristotle said were available
for this inductive form. In general, as the overall nature of rhetoric
dictates, the materials are likely to be probabilities, though they
need not be. "The enthymeme and the example must, then, deal
with what is in the main contingent."[33]

But such a general description is of only limited use, and in
ii.20 Aristotle is definite:

> This form of argument has two varieties; one consisting in the mention
> of actual past facts, the other in the invention of facts by the speaker.
> Of the latter, again, there are two varieties, the illustrative parallel and
> the fable (e.g. the fables of Aesop, or those from Libya).[34]

Four illustrations of the use of example follow. The first, which
presents two historic instances, infers directly that a similar outcome is likely "If therefore the present king seizes Egypt, he also
will cross, and therefore we must not let him."[35] The speaker
makes no assertion that he has examined all instances, and he does
not place a generalization between the instances and the conclusion. The second illustration, called an illustrative parallel and
attributed to Socrates, begins by stating the conclusion and then
presents two parallel situations in which the course opposite to the
conclusion obviously is wrong. This illustration also contains no
claim that all possible parallels have been examined, nor does it
include the generalization under which the conclusion falls. The
third and the fourth illustrations are fables about animals that
conclude by applying the outcome of the tale to the proposition
that the speaker is trying to prove. "Fables are suitable for
addresses to popular assemblies," Aristotle observes, "and they
have one advantage — they are comparatively easy to invent,
whereas it is hard to find parallels among actual past events."[36]
However, ". . .while it is easier to supply parallels by inventing
fables, it is more valuable for the political speaker to supply them
by quoting what has actually happened, since in most respects the
future will be like what the past has been."[37]

From this treatment two important inferences are possible:

33. *Ibid.,* i.2.1357^{a}14 -15.
34. 1393^{a}26 -30.
35. 1393^{b}3 -4.
36. 1394 ^{a}2 -4.
37. 1394^{a}6 -9.

(1) Both the variety and the kinds of materials considered suitable for the example suggest that it is a form of argument that is usable in many circumstances. (2) Since several forms are permissible, the speaker can make choices according to his rhetorical needs. The movement from the known to the conclusion may or may not proceed through an intervening verbalized generalization, the speaker has the option of arranging the elements of the total argument deductively (stating the conclusion first), and, as in the second illustration, the speaker may combine example with an argument through opposites. Example, thus, is a device of great versatility.

Values and Further Uses

From this flexibility and the other attributes already presented arise the values and the uses. The example clarifies, dramatizes,[38] serves as a base for enthymemes, has a special but limited and poorly explained role in demonstration, and is a type of reasoning of considerable importance in rhetoric. Illuminating these values and functions — and of special interest because these expansions suggest that Aristotle considered the example a significant tool for the rhetorical practicioner — are passages of instruction. In ii.25 Aristotle considers the refutation of enthymemes depending on examples,[39] and in three places he correlates the values of example with each of the types of oratory and explains why it is particularly adapted to deliberative speaking.[40] ". . .we judge of future events," he points out, "by divination from past events."[41]

The most detailed instruction about using the example is

---

38. Charles Sears Baldwin sees this function as the most important — a view with which the writer disagrees. "Example includes analogy, both from history and from fiction, with specific mention of fables. In this wide sense, including mere illustration, it means little more than vividness of presentation through the concrete and specific; but that its persuasive value far exceeds its logical cogency no one doubts who knows audiences." *Ancient Rhetoric and Poetic* (New York: The Macmillan Company, 1924), p.20.

39. $1403^a 5$ -9.

40. *Rhet.* i.2.$1356^b 18$ -24; i.9.$1368^a 29$ -33; iii.17. $1418^a 2$ -3.

41. *Ibid.,* i.9.$1368^a 30$.

the passage that closes ii.20. Aristotle begins here by identifying the two general uses — as the means of proof when the enthymeme is not possible and as a supplement to the enthymeme:

> When we are unable to argue by Enthymeme, we must try to demonstrate our point by this method of example, and to convince our hearers thereby. If we can argue by Enthymeme, we should use our Examples as subsequent supplementary evidence. They should not precede the Enthymemes: that will give the argument an inductive air, which only rarely suits the conditions of speech-making. If they follow the enthymemes, they have the effect of witnesses giving evidence, and this always tells. For the same reason, if you put your examples first you must give a large number of them; if you put them last, a single one is sufficient; even a single witness will serve if he is a good one.[42]

Summary and Conclusion

Example and induction are two different forms in demonstration, and the treatments of the two in the *Rhetoric* also are separate. In places, though, Aristotle refers to example as "rhetorical induction" and as the counterpart of the induction of dialectic. Characterized by its basic qualities, example is a form of reasoning that moves from known to unknown, that functions within a single genus or order, and that moves from an individual instance to a conclusion about some other individual instance either with or without an intervening expressed generalization. In rhetoric the material ordinarily is within the realm of probabilities, the number of instances almost always is less than the total, and the argument may be an analogy of relations or one of substantive cases. The example may be a form of reasoning by itself, it may be the basis for an enthymeme, or it may strengthten the believability of an enthymeme. Used as an argument, if often gains strength through the presence of related rhetorical devices.

That the *Rhetoric* gives a considerable amount of space to the example is proof that it has an important, though subordinate, place in Aristotle's system of communication. Situations, the nature of the speaker, and the type of oratory vary, and the precise function of example depends upon these three and other considerations. ". . .in some oratorical styles examples prevail, in

42. 1394[a]9 -17.

others enthymemes; and in like manner, some orators are better at the former and some at the latter. Speeches that rely on examples are as persuasive as the other kind, but those which rely on enthymemes excite the louder applause."[43]

ANALOGY

One serious limitation was common to both induction and the relatively flexible example. The restriction of their scopes to instances within the same genus failed to provide for some types of imaginative, creative thought. A third type, therefore, was required for a fully developed inductive system. Aristotle perceived this deficiency, recognized the existence of analogy in Greek discourse, and gave it his approval.

Nowhere, however, does he define analogy or treat it in detail or systematically. Once more, therefore, a coherent statement is possible only through an analysis of separated passages, the drawing of inferences, and the synthesizing of ideas. Fortunately, the meaning of analogy in Aristotle is consistent and is essentially the same as it is today. The distinctive purposes in the writings, as in modern popular usage, are to generalize and differentiate when simpler and more direct methods are inapplicable.

> Likeness should be studied, first, in the case of things belonging to different genera, the formulae being "A:B=C:D"... and "As A is in B, so is C in D".... Practice is more especially needed in regard to terms that are far apart; for in the case of the rest, we shall be more easily able to see in one glance the points of likeness.[44]

Further references expand and illuminate this general statement. The *Metaphysics* refers to analogy in a number of places as a possible means of finding likenesses and differences,[45] the *Poetics* presents it as the basis of metaphor,[46] and the *Posterior Analytics* cites its usefulness in classification when other methods fail[47] and

43. *Ibid.*, i.2.1356[b]20 -24.
44. *Top.* i.17.108[a]7 -14. See also *Meta.* ix.6.1048[b]4 -8.
45. v.6.1016[b]32 -1017[a]3; v.9.1018[a]12 -14; xii.4.1070[a]31 -[b]26; xii.5. 1071[a]4 -36.
46. Ch. 21.1457[b]7 -19. The translation is by Ingram Bywater.
47. ii.14.98[a]20 -23.

offers the rule that "connexions requiring proof which are identical by analogy have middles also analogous."[48] The *Topics* in a passage on likeness as an inductive form suggests that the dialectician establish what is easy and then transfer the proof to the conclusion that he is trying to sustain.[49] In following this recommendation the reasoner, of course, is proceeding through analogy.

Generalizing successfully when instances are widely spaced, seeing likenesses that transcend the genus, and drawing conclusions from a pair of related ratios, thus, characterize Aristotle's analogy. These qualities, it is interesting to note, constitute an early counterpart to the twentieth century theory that analogy is critical to creativity.[50] True enough, Aristotle formulated nothing in this area comprehensive enough to be called theory, but numerous brief passages indicate that to him analogy was a source of insight. Elsewhere he makes his principal statement on insight when he describes how one grasps the universal through induction (see pp. 59-60).

A FORTIORI

Completing the group of inductive forms is *a fortiori,* which Aristotle discusses by name in one place, presents in effect in several parts of his works, and illustrates in his own writing. *A fortiori,* nevertheless, is not a major logical form.

The specific presentation, in the *Rhetoric* ii.23, is the fourth *topos* :

> Another line of proof is the *a fortiori.* Thus it may be argued that if even the gods are not omniscient, certainly human beings are not. The principle here is that, if a quality does not in fact exist where it is *more* likely to exist, it clearly does not exist where it is *less* likely. . . . Or it may be urged that, if a thing is not true where it is more likely, it is not true where it is less likely; or that, if it is true where it is less likely, it is true where it is more likely.[51]

48. ii.17.99^{a}16.

49. i.18.108^{b}12 -19.

50. For example, see Elwood Murray and J. L. Stewart, "Analogue Bases for Research in Creativity," *Journal of Communication,* XIII (Dec., 1963), 246 -251.

51. 1397^{b}11 -18.

What this passage creates is a paradigm of three elements —
an alleged or hypothesized act, a less favorable circumstance, and a
more favorable circumstance. This meaning has lasted to the
modern day without alterations by intervening scholars. Virtually
unknown at present, though, is the four-element *a fortiori* that the
following passage in the *Topics* describes in an application of the
argument of degrees:

> Moreover: If two predicates be attributed to two subjects, then if the
> one which is more usually thought to belong to the one subject does
> not belong, neither does the remaining predicate belong to the re-
> maining subject; or, if the one which is less usually thought to belong
> to the one subject does belong, so too does the remaining predicate to
> the remaining subject.[52]

This four-element form poses obvious difficulties, but its restora-
tion to rhetorical treatments of *a fortiori* would give speakers and
writers an additional resource.

Other passages on this inductive form neither expand the
theory nor improve the clarity, but the appearance in the *Rhetoric*
of at least eight examples or descriptions of *a fortiori* versions of
the argument of degree[53] indicates that Aristotle found it useful.
Perhaps the most interesting of these citations is the following:

> Every one honours the wise. Thus the Parisians have honoured Archilo-
> chus, in spite of his bitter tongue; the Chians Homer, though he was
> not their countryman; the Mytilenaeans Sappho, though she was a
> woman; the Lacedaemonians actually made Chilon a member of their
> senate, though they are the least literary of men; the Italian Greeks
> honoured Pythagoras; the inhabitants of Lampsacus gave public burial
> to Anaxagoras, though he was an alien, and honour him even to this
> day.[54]

The function of *a fortiori,* to conclude, is not so much the
creating of new knowledge, though in a sense it does so, as it is the
establishing of the reasonableness of a preselected conclusion. This
function Aristotle understood, employed, and set forth for his
successors.

---

52. ii.10.115^{a}11 -14. For examples of the three-element format see ii.
10.115^{a}6 -11 and v.8.138^{a}3 -29.

53. i.13.1375^{a}12-13;   i.13.1375^{a}18 -20;   ii.5.1382^{b}14 -17;   ii.
19.1392^{b}5 -12; ii.19.1392^{b}15 -16; ii.23.1397^{b}27 -29; ii.23.1397^{b}32 -^{a}3.

54. ii.23.1398^{b}9 -15.

CONCLUSION

Combined, the four inductive forms (induction labeled as such, example, analogy, and *a fortiori*) constitute a varied, workable instrument useful both in reasoning to new conclusions and in supporting preselected positions. This instrument, with suitable adaptations, is useful in demonstration, dialectic, and rhetoric. The treatment probably reflects accurately the inductive practices of the Athenian society that Aristotle knew, and it constitutes a body of theory that has largely survived to the present.

In no age has induction been a precise, highly developed logical form, and Aristotle's treatment shares in these universal inadequacies. The careful study of the rather large number of scattered, sketchy passages, nevertheless, yields a more extensive and more coherent body of material than most scholars would expect.

The following conclusions are based on both an analysis of Aristotle's illustrations of inductive forms and on an examination of his explicit, scattered statements:

1. For a full view of Aristotle's induction, the scholar must examine passages pertaining to all levels and branches of the logical system. He also must consider materials on example, analogy, and *a fortiori* as well as those on induction so labeled.

2. Induction is more than the process of attaining scientific certainty through complete enumeration. It also is the process of generalizing on the basis of qualities common to species, a largely unstructured process leading to insight, and the process in dialectic and rhetoric of showing probabilities by combining examples with various rhetorical devices.

3. Besides the uses and values already implied, induction when employed alone is valuable for its clarity and persuasiveness, for its probative force in a variety of dialectical situations, for its service as scientific proof when deduction is impossible, and for its usefulness in apprehending attributes.

4. Induction is of unquestionable importance as the source of the immediate premises from which deduction proceeds.

5. Example and induction are two different forms in demonstration, and the treatments of the two in the *Rhetoric* also are separate.

6. Example is a form of reasoning that functions within a

single genus or order and that moves from an individual instance to a conclusion about some other individual instance either with or without an intervening expressed generalization. The modern mathematical analogy is included in Aristotle's treatment of example as a rhetorical resource.

7. In rhetoric the example may be a form of reasoning by itself, it may be the basis for an enthymeme, or it may strengthen the believability of an enthymeme.

8. Analogy in Aristotle serves to round out his inductive system by providing for reasoning when instances are not within the same genus.

9. *A fortiori* is an inductive form whose primary function is to heighten the probability of a conclusion.

10. Aristotle presents both a three-element and a four-element paridigm of *a fortiori*. The former has been transmitted to the present day without significant change, but the latter does not appear in modern books on speech and communication.

CHAPTER 5

Conclusion: An Appraisal and a Summary

Aristotle's induction and deduction combined form a logical system that is an important part of the cultural heritage of Western civilization and that is a significant factor in the communication acts of modern man. "The matter of the *Prior Analytics*," writes Alexander Grant, "has become the common property of all modern books on logic. And scarcely anything has had to be detracted from or added to what Aristotle wrote upon the syllogism. His was the proud distinction of having discovered and fully drawn out the laws under which the mind acts in deductive reasoning."[1] Such testimony is not uncommon; indeed, the complaint of Aristotle's detractors is likely to be that he is too influential.

Without logic man could devise no message worthy of his humanness, and without logic he could not inform and persuade others. Through the enthymeme Aristotle contributed to communication a practical method of bending deduction to the ends of the persuader, through the syllogism he presented an elaborate and workable system of finding and testing truth, and through induction he provided forms that complement and support both of these two deductive functions.

Logic as a constituent of the process of message formation is of unquestionable significance in any age, and Aristotle's treatment by its breadth, systematic analysis, and profoundness must be appraised the most influential in the history of mankind if not, even 2300 years after its creation, still the most thorough and astute.

For Aristotle's logical system brought deduction, including the treatment of causes, to a level not yet surpassed, and the

1. "Aristotle" in *Encyclopedia Britannica: A Dictionary of Arts, Sciences, and General Literature,* 9th ed., Vol.II (New York: Samuel L. Hall, 1878), p. 516.

limited nature of his consideration of induction can be at least partly extenuated. Combined, the coverage of the two is comprehensive, and the approach brings together theoretical brilliance and practical common sense. Properly applied, Aristotle's teachings guide the communicator not only in the disciplined, systematic search for truth but also in the nimble manipulation of probabilities, which by necessity are usually the substance in dialectical and rhetorical situations. In the logical system Aristotle holds out a clear, brilliant view of a completely accurate science of reasoning; but also realizing that the ideal is not always obtainable, he advises on the ways of doing the best that circumstances permit. Thus, his system covers the entire range of communicative situations.

As a set of methods of analysis, Aristotle's writings are without equal. The modern reasoner using Aristotle as a guide has the means of exploring a topic systematically, creatively, and in depth. In the detailed consideration of the formulation of premises Aristotle shows how to turn a problem area this way and that; he also shows how to manipulate premises into forms that may lead to increased clarity or even to an insight that otherwise would not occur.

Limitations, however, exist. The contribution to induction is disappointing, and dialectic is not an entirely satisfactory method of testing the first premise. A faulty first premise, of course, means that a conclusion, though formally valid, may be wrong in fact – a possibility that Aristotle acknowledges when he says that a reasoned conclusion that is inconsistent with reality is not true.[2] Perhaps a still more serious limitation, though, is the very vastness and complexity of the whole. Few can master the system, and its complete application is beyond the patience, if not the capability, of most. Simplifications and popularizations, however, exist, and thus Aristotle's teachings in part are widely available.

On the positive side, besides the great contributions to

2. He makes the point repeatedly that conclusions reached by reasoning should be consistent with reality. See the *Posterior Analytics* i.9.76^{a}28 -30, i.13.78^{a}22 -24, i.13.78^{b}31 -32, i.14.79^{a}23 -24, and i.27.87^{a}30 -31; see also the *Nicomachean Ethics* vi.7.1141^{a}16 -17. The translation of the *N. Ethics* is by W. D. Ross.

theory and method, there is a flexibility, broadness, tolerance, and common sense that stand as example and warning to any modern theorist. Contrary to general belief, Aristotle did not regard demonstration as the only means of securing knowledge.[3] Moreover, his system provides for intermediates and continua,[4] includes both the fact and the reasoned fact,[5] and even in demonstration recognizes that in some circumstances something less than absoluteness can be sensible.[6]

So the contributions are both direct and indirect, obvious and subtle, theoretical and practical. The system, despite some deficiencies, has survived for twenty-three centuries and remains useful and dominant.

3. "The contention of some... that all truths are demonstrable is mistaken." *Post. An.* i.23.84^{a}32 -33. The translation is by G. R. G. Mure. See also *On the Soul* iii.7 and iii.8 for sense perception as a source of particulars and the *N. Ethics* vi.3 -7 for descriptions of science, art, practical wisdom, intuitive reason, and philosophic wisdom as intellectual methods. See *supra,* pp. 58-59, for the indispensable role of induction.

4. "Quantity is either discrete or continuous.... Instances of discrete quantities are number and speech; of continuous, lines, surfaces, solids, and besides these, time and place." *Categories* Ch. 6.4^{b}20-24. The translation is by E. M. Edghill. A similar statement appears for qualities (*Ibid.,* Ch. 8.10^{b}26 -28), and Aristotle analyzes in considerable detail the quantities and the qualities that have variations in degree and those that do not. Blackness and whiteness as well as badness and goodness are among the contraries that have intermediates. *Ibid.,* Ch. 10.12^{a}10 -25.

5. *Supra,* p. 102 and note 2.

6. The *Posterior Analytics* provides for reasoning (called atomic) when no middle term exists (i.15.79^{a}33 -^{b}44) and for middle terms that are only general rules. "Some occurrences are universal (for they are, or come-to-be what they are, always and in every case); others again are not always what they are but only as a general rule.... In the case of such connexions the middle term must be a general rule.... So connexions which embody a general rule.... will also derive from immediate basic premisses." ii.12. 96^{a}8 -19. A statement by W. D. Ross also is relevant: "It is noteworthy that, while Aristotle conceives of demonstration in the strict sense as proceeding from premises that are necessarily true to conclusions that are necessarily true, he recognizes demonstration (in a less strict sense, of course) as capable of proceeding from premises for the most part true to similar conclusions." *Aristotle's Prior and Posterior Analytics* (New York: Oxford University Press, 1949), p. 74.

Such a system is well worth studying, and the preceding chapters should have served (1) to provide a clear, understandable introduction to a topic that is highly complex in the original and (2) to develop some views and emphases that have not been common in scholarly analyses.

To realize the first objective, the writer has sought to select, order, and phrase ideas clearly. Taking up in progression terms, premises, and the syllogism is an attempt to clarify the structure of deduction, and the analysis of the substance of demonstration follows an order also carefully calculated. Still another contribution to clarification is the attention given to definitions of technical terms that are important to understanding Aristotle's logical system. Chapter 2 contains succinct explanations of *predication, universal, particular, indefinite, necessary, assertoric, contingent, hypothesis, postulate, primary, commensurately universal, figure, mode, contrary, contradictory, conversion,* and reductio ad impossible. Definitions of still other concepts appear in other chapters.

As for the second objective, positive assertions are risky, for the vastness of the Aristotelian literature makes it unlikely that any conclusion is entirely new. The following statements, some of which possess some newness, close this volume by summarizing the most important ideas:

1. *Likenesses and differences.* In structure the logics for demonstration, for dialectic, and for rhetoric are alike, but in subject matter and in the rigor of the requirements governing manipulation they are different.

2. *The role of causation.* In deduction for science (or demonstration) causation is a safeguard against a possible separation of reasoning from reality. In science a conclusion must meet the test of proper cause-effect relation as well as the test of correct structure.

3. *The content of demonstration.* The two primary topics for demonstration are whether ———— is a fact and whether ———— exists. The two secondary topics are cause and essence. The materials used in demonstration are (*a*) axioms applicable to all science and (*b*) substantive statements for the particular science to which the syllogism pertains.

4. *The role of definition.* Definition is vital to the whole

process of deduction because the true subject matter of the syllogism is the *ideas* that words represent and not the words themselves. Aristotle's writings anticipate many of the formulations of semanticists and general semanticists.

5. *The nature of demonstrative premises.* They must be true, necessary, essential, and commensurately universal; they should contain causes, be empirically true, and be closer to the basic propositions than is the conclusion. The movement in deductive reasoning is from a position relatively close to the first principle to one that is relatively further removed.

6. *The difference between* necessity *and* essentiality. Necessity means invariable and true in every instance; essentiality refers to inevitability. The relation of predicate to subject is *per se* in essentiality, not merely *de omni* as in necessity. Whereas necessity is determined empirically, essentiality is determined abstractly and formally.

7. *The obtaining of premises.* Science and the two nonsciences differ in the way that premises are obtained. In the former the reasoner lays down the premise according to formal rules but without any obligation to consult with others; in rhetoric and dialectic interactions with other human beings largely determine premises.

8. *Limitations on deductive manipulation.* In both demonstration and nonscientific discourse the reasoner may form new premises by manipulating old ones, but the limitations for the two kinds of deduction are not the same. In science the limitation is what formal rules permit; in rhetoric, what the listener will accept; in dialectic, what the procedural rules approve.

9. *The nature of the enthymeme.* The enthymeme is not correctly defined as an elided syllogism, and other misconceptions have arisen through carelessness. Aristotle's statements about qualities *usually* true have been misconstrued as meaning "*always* true."

10. *Signs.* Aristotle's inclusion of reasoning from signs is indicative of his careful observation of the mental processes of his fellow men. He neglected, however, to consider the critical point of whether outward appearance bears an invariable relation to inner quality. His analysis of signs as fallible creates a false dichotomy, for this form of reasoning is viewed more accurately as a continuum extending from coincidental relation to certainty.

11. *The comprehensiveness of Aristotle's induction.* A full view of this second part of the total system requires an examination of passages on example, analogy, and *a fortiori* as well as those on "induction." Such a view leads to the conclusion that Aristotle in this area is more comprehensive and systematic than has been believed generally.

12. *The flexibility of Aristotle's induction.* The strict requirement that induction include all instances applies only to demonstrative reasoning. Aristotle's system includes both reasoning based on species and generalizing through insight – an outcome that may occur after examining any particular instance in a series.

13. *Example.* The definition of *example* as "rhetorical induction" is inaccurate, for example also has a limited place in demonstration. Aristotle's example, which is reasoning from one particular to another, is comparable to today's literal analogy.

14. *Analogy and modern creativity.* Whereas induction and example are restricted to reasoning within a particular genus, analogy may deal in more than one genus. Aristotle's analogy is a forerunner of some modern theorizing on creativity.

15. A fortiori. Aristotle's *a fortiori* includes a three-element paradigm that survives unchanged in modern writings and a four-element paradigm that has not survived.

The scope and the complexity of Aristotle's system will stand as a challenge to every generation of scholars. No volume, including the present one, will ever exhaust the opportunities for analysis and synthesis.

BIBLIOGRAPHY

Works by Aristotle

Categories, tr. E. M. Edghill.
Metaphysics, tr. W. D. Ross.
Nicomachean Ethics, tr. W. D. Ross.
On Interpretation, tr. E. M. Edghill.
On Sophistical Refutatations, tr. W. A. Pickard-Cambridge.
On the Soul, tr. J. A. Smith.
Physics, tr. R. P. Hardie and R. K. Gaye.
Posterior Analytics, tr. G. R. G. Mure.
Prior Analytics, tr. A. J. Jenkinson.
Rhetoric, tr. Lane Cooper.
(———), tr. W. Rhys Roberts.
(———), tr. J. E. C. Welldon.
Topics, tr. W. A. Pickard-Cambridge.

Other Works

Atkins, J. W. H. *Literary Criticism in Antiquity,* Vol. I. Cambridge, England: At the University Press, 1934.

Baldwin, Charles S. *Ancient Rhetoric and Poetic.* New York: The Macmillan Company, 1924.

Bitzer, Lloyd F. "Aristotle's Enthymeme Revisited," *Quarterly Journal of Speech,* XLV (Dec., 1959), 399 -408.

Cooper, Lane. "The *Rhetoric* of Aristotle," *Quarterly Journal of Speech,* XXI (Feb., 1935), 10 -18.

Cope, E. M. *An Introduction to Aristotle's Rhetoric.* London, 1867.

Copleston, Frederick. *A History of Philosophy,* Vol. I. Garden City, N. Y.: Image Books, 1962.

Grant, Alexander. "Aristotle," in *Encyclopedia Britannica: A Dictionary of Arts, Sciences, and General Literature,* 9th ed., Vol. II. New York: Samuel L. Hall, 1878, pp.510 -523.

Grene, Marjorie. *A Portrait of Aristotle.* Chicago: University of Chicago Press, 1963.

Grote, George. *Aristotle,* ed. Alexander Bain and G. C. Robertson. London, 1883.

Hunt, Everett Lee. "Plato and Aristotle on Rhetoric and Rhetoricians," in Raymond F. Howes, ed., *Historical Studies of Rhetoric and Rhetoricians.* Ithaca, N. Y.: Cornell University Press, 1961, pp. 19 -70.

Jaeger, Werner. *Aristotle: Fundamentals of the History of His Development,* tr. Richard Robinson. Oxford: At the Clarendon Press, 1948.

Kennedy, George. *The Art of Persuasion in Greece.* Princeton, N.J.: Princeton University Press, 1963.

McBurney, James H. "The Place of the Enthymeme in Rhetorical Theory," *Speech Monographs,* III (1936), 49 -74.

McKeon, Richard. "Aristotle's Conception of Language and the Arts of Language," *Classical Philology,* XLI (Oct., 1946), 193 -206; and XLII (Jan., 1947), 21 -59.

(———) , "Aristotle's Conception of the Development and the Nature of Scientific Method," *Journal of the History of Ideas,* VIII (Jan., 1947), 3 -44.

(———), *Introduction to Aristotle.* New York: Modern Library, 1947.

Mudd, Charles S. "The Enthymeme and Logical Validity," *Quarterly Journal of Speech,* XLV (Dec., 1959), 409 -414.

Mure, G. R. G. *Aristotle.* New York: Oxford University Press, 1932.

Organ, Troy. *Index to Aristotle.* Princeton, N. J.: Princeton University Press, 1949.

Randall, John H., Jr. *Aristotle.* New York: Columbia University Press, 1960.

Roberts, W. Rhys. *Greek Rhetoric and Literary Criticism.* New York: Longmans, Green and Co., 1928.

Ross., W. D. *Aristotle.* London: Methuen & Co., 1949.

INDEX

GRAZER BEITRÄGE

ZEITSCHRIFT FÜR DIE KLASSISCHE ALTERTUMSWISSENSCHAFT

hrg. von

Franz Stoessl, Eugen Dönt, Gerhard Petersmann

Die GRAZER BEITRÄGE erscheinen jährlich mit mindestens 1 Band. Bestellungen werden an den Buchhandel oder direkt an den Verlag erbeten.

Manuskripte werden an einen der Herausgeber, Institut für Klassische Philologie, Universität Graz, A-8010 Graz, Austria erbeten. Beiträge werden in englischer, französischer, italienischer und deutscher Sprache angenommen. Der Verlag stellt jedem Mitarbeiter 25 Separata unentgeltlich zur Verfügung; Beiträge über 8 Druckseiten werden mit dem Umschlagblatt der Zeitschrift versehen.

Beiträge können nur in druckfertigem Zustand übernommen werden, griechische Zitate mögen nur maschinschriftlich in das Manuskript aufgenommen werden. Aus drucktechnischen Gründen wird gebeten, Anmerkungen in fortlaufender Numerierung dem Beitrag getrennt beizulegen.

Es wird ersucht, dem Beitrag eine kurze Zusammenfassung von 5-10 Maschinschreibzeilen beizugeben.

Die GRAZER BEITRÄGE nehmen Buchbesprechungen auf; Rezensionsexemplare werden an einen der Herausgeber erbeten.

EDITIONS RODOPI NV

KEIZERSGRACHT 302-304

AMSTERDAM – THE NETHERLANDS